Freeing tangled hearts

Freeing tangled hearts

Dolores Kimball

PUBLISHING WITH A MISSION

EP BOOKS
Faverdale North
Darlington
DL3 0PH, England

www.epbooks.org
sales@epbooks.org

EP BOOKS are distributed in the USA by:
JPL Distribution
3741 Linden Avenue Southeast
Grand Rapids, MI 49548.

E-mail: orders@jpldistribution.com
Tel: 877.683.6935

First published 2013

British Library Cataloguing in Publication Data available
ISBN: 978-0-85234-915-1

A free downloadable study guide for this book is available from
www.freeingtangledhearts.com

Contents

To Tom,
whose wisdom, insights, love for God,
and encouragement made this book possible.

Introduction

The principles for freeing the tangled heart became clear to me after reading literally thousands of questions from women all over the world in my position as Managing Editor of GotQuestions.org, a Bible question and answer internet ministry, which has received and answered over 300,000 questions in its ten-year history. After a few years, I began to realize that the heart cries of women in Africa were the same as those in the U.S., and those of women in Asia were no different from those in Europe. I saw patterns emerging in the questions from women, patterns that indicate women everywhere have the same issues — issues of the heart and the things that tangle it. The principles in this book, based entirely on the Scriptures, will help women tame the jumble of thoughts, feelings and attitudes that tangle our hearts and make a mess of our lives.

But this is not a 'how-to' book. It does not contain cheerleader phrases and advice. You know what I mean by cheerleader phrases: 'You can do it!'; 'Make a decision!'; 'Commit yourself!';

'Make a vow to God!'; 'Just speak words of faith into your life!'
I will tell you from the outset that you haven't the capacity to
free your tangled heart. If you could, you wouldn't be looking
for a book on the subject. This is not a book about what you
can do. It's a book about what God has already done. But these
principles absolutely do work, and if you or those you counsel
will apply them in the power of the Holy Spirit, you will find
hearts untangling in an amazing way.

Women's hearts become tangled and strangled in ways that are
different from men. Our doubts and fears are very personal. We
doubt our ability to be loved, to be good mothers, to maintain
successful and meaningful relationships, and we doubt our
own worth and value. We fear losing our attractiveness and
our independence as we age. We have fears about children —
having them, not having them, what will happen to them and
become of them. And we fear doing the wrong thing or making
the wrong decisions. Then there are doubts about God, our own
salvation, and our worth in his eyes.

Jesus said, 'Apart [i.e., separated] from me you can do nothing'
(John 15:5). So the first step in untangling the heart is to have a
reasonable assurance of the reality of our own salvation. Unless
we are in Christ, we have no hope of untangling our hearts
because we simply have no connection to the power source.
A lamp on the table may be beautiful and decorative, but it is
functionally worthless when night falls if it is not plugged in.
Only when it is attached to the power source can it shed light
and warmth into the darkness. So it is with women who don't
have the Holy Spirit as their power source — they are unable
to pierce the darkness of the tangled heart. So examining
ourselves to see if we are *truly in the faith* is the first step in the

untangling process because — and this is very important — no amount of advice or counseling will solve your problems if your biggest problem is that you are separated from God.

The World War II generation knew some things about war against Nazism that Christian women must recognize about the spiritual war we wage if our hearts are to be untangled. They knew who the enemy was and how to defeat him, and they knew they were in it for the long haul. War against the enemy of our souls is real; he is powerful and relentless, so we must be totally engaged in the battle, and changes in our thinking and our actions are necessary to defeat him. But God has given us the full armor, everything we need to wage the war. Women so often lose the battle daily by listening to the enemy as he tangles up our hearts by manipulating our thoughts and emotions, instead of listening to God and living by faith. Demonic forces constantly feed our fears and doubts because they know that will weaken our faith, and their primary theater of operations is the culture we live in. They don't have to work on us personally; the culture they control does their dirty work for them. So gearing up for the battle involves *understanding who the enemy is*, how he fights, and how he is defeated.

Part of the battle women wage every day is the battle of our emotions. The goal is to *manage our emotions* instead of letting them manage us. The victory over our emotions enables us to recognize when they are lying to us, and to know what to do with negative emotions like fear, doubt, guilt, anger, bitterness and envy (each of which is addressed in a separate chapter) in order to keep them from ruling our lives and tangling our hearts. Negative emotions do not have power over us. They are part of the old person we were before Christ remade us into entirely new creations. He enables us to be 'more than conquerors through him who loved us' (Rom. 8:37). No negative emotion or thought can withstand his power.

The fourth in our five-point cure for a tangled heart is the advice of a famous Welsh preacher and counselor Dr Martyn Lloyd-Jones: *refuse to think about yourself.* There is one inviolable rule in life: 'Those who obsess about themselves will never be happy in any circumstance. Those who obsess about God will find joy in all circumstances.' When our thoughts begin and end with us — the norm in our unhealthy psychological generation — we live in a constant state of defeat because we are controlled by subjective feelings centered on ourselves, rather than objective truth centered on God. What we continually forget, if we ever learned it in the first place, is that we are dead, 'crucified with Christ' (Gal. 2:20). The old person we were, with all its sin and hurts and misery, is dead and buried. We have to resist the temptation to keep digging up the coffin.

If we take to heart Lloyd-Jones's admonition to refuse to think about ourselves, we must realize we can't do it by determining not to think about ourselves, because by thinking about not thinking about ourselves, we end up doing just that. Negative thought patterns which tangle our hearts can easily become an ingrained habit. But if we replace the negative thoughts with positive thoughts about God and his truth, we will find that the negative, damaging thoughts will simply melt away. We put off negative emotions and thoughts by *putting on truths about God from his Word*, beginning with an understanding of the absolute sovereignty of a compassionate, merciful, faithful, loving God. Faith falters and the flesh prevails when women lose a biblical perspective on the nature of God. To be reminded that he is 'in his holy temple', ruling and reigning in sovereign majesty, ordering and superintending the affairs of his world with actual hands-on management, so that not a sparrow falls to the ground without his notice, is the food that strengthens faith.

These are the five principles that untangle hearts. They absolutely do work and I hope that by the time you've finished reading this book, you are as confident of that as I am, not because I'm telling you so, but because God is telling you so. My prayer is that you join women from all over the world who have discovered the thrill of an untangled heart and a life filled with peace and joy.

1

'Tangled and mangled and strangled.

Oh my!'

S tevie Nicks and Tom Petty have asked me to stop draggin' their
heart around, and the Backstreet Boys tell me they would
never break my heart. Frank Sinatra wanted to remain young at
heart and Dee Brown wants her heart buried at Wounded Knee.
Joseph Conrad shuddered at the Heart of Darkness and the hero
of Edgar Allen Poe's story was betrayed by his Telltale Heart.
Proverbs 4:23 warns us to guard the heart 'for it is the wellspring
of life'. Jeremiah 17:9 assures us that our hearts are deceitful and
desperately wicked, and David is described as a man after God's
own heart (1 Sam. 13:14).

There are a vast number of books, songs, poems, quotes and
Bible verses about hearts, indicating that people are very
concerned with matters of the heart. Hearts are described in
story and song as broken, hard, soft, cheating, faithful, joyful,
full, empty, merry or melancholy. We can be brokenhearted,

downhearted, fainthearted or wholehearted. In the following chapters, we are going to look at hearts that are tangled and strangled, crushed and wounded, and what God says about how to begin to untangle them. If your own heart is tangled, the things you read here will help you to begin untangling it. If your heart is not tangled, but you know someone who needs help untangling her heart, you will find these principles immensely helpful in ministering to her. Whether you are struggling with a tangled heart or you are involved in or interested in counseling others, you will be encouraged to know that these principles, based entirely on the Scriptures, have helped many people to live happier and more productive lives in Christ.

What is a 'tangled heart'?

The word 'heart' in all its forms appears over a thousand times in the NIV. Mostly the Bible refers to the heart as the seat of emotions, intellect, will and personality. It also encompasses the nature, which is either a fallen nature or a redeemed nature. So the heart is the total person — all of what is inside us, not the organs, but the deep well of feelings, thoughts, ideas, desires and memories that make up the person we are. Proverbs 27:19 says, 'As water reflects a face, so a man's heart reflects the man.' What is in our hearts reflects who we are, just as looking in a mirror reflects what we look like.

The word 'tangle' is defined as a confused, intertwined mass, a jumbled or confused state or condition, or a state of bewilderment. Think of a hopelessly tangled knot, the kind a child gets when she falls asleep with chewing gum in her mouth and it ends up in her hair. So a tangled heart occurs when the mind, emotions, will and personality become an intertwined, jumbled mass of confusion and bewilderment. Pretty descriptive, isn't it? The sad fact is that millions of women, many of them Christians, go through life like that every day! Is it any wonder there are nervous breakdowns, prescriptions for Valium written by the millions, and desperate housewives all over the place? Does this describe you, or anyone you know?

What does a person with a tangled heart look like?

Remember that the heart is all that we are internally, and tangled means confused and knotted. So the woman with the tangled heart is all knotted up inside, making decisions and coming to conclusions influenced by that confused condition. And the woman with a tangled heart usually reveals that heart through her words. Remember Jesus' words in Luke 6:45? 'The good man brings good things out of the good stored up in his heart, and the evil man brings evil things out of the evil stored up in his heart. For out of the overflow of his heart his mouth speaks.' Our words are a reflection of what is in our hearts. Isn't that obvious? Unless we are consummate hypocrites and experts at hiding what is in our hearts, sooner or later it's going to come pouring out of our mouths, and this is especially true for women.

If you sit in any coffee shop near two women and eavesdrop on their conversation, in minutes you will discover what is in their hearts. I don't know what it is about sitting in Starbucks that causes us to pour out our hearts to one another. Maybe it's something they put in the coffee. In any case, out of the abundance of tangled thoughts, feelings and attitudes in our hearts, ours words flow day in and day out. As women, there is something about the way we are 'wired' that compels us to pour forth verbally what is stored up in our hearts.

Women with tangled hearts often reveal their confusion in their appearance, as well as their conversation. Some of us are good at hiding what is in our hearts, but most of us are more obvious than that. The old expression 'she wears her heart on her sleeve' really describes a person whose feelings are apparent to others. The average woman wears her tangled heart on her sleeve. Proverbs 15:13 tells us that 'A happy heart makes the face cheerful, but heartache crushes the spirit.' When our hearts are burdened down by the fears, doubts and guilt that are so common today, we cannot help but reveal it to the world through our appearance. There is a great sympathy between the heart and the body. The heartache that 'crushes the spirit' also lowers the eyes to the ground, slumps the shoulders, pales the complexion, and dulls the expression. While the medical profession might tell us no one really dies from a broken heart, there is no doubt that a person's mental and emotional well-being have a significant impact on the ability to recover from illness. Proverbs 18:14 reminds us that 'A man's spirit sustains him in sickness, but a crushed spirit who can bear?' Sadly, millions of Christian women bear the burden of a crushed spirit and a tangled heart.

Perhaps even worse than the effects of the tangled heart on our appearance, health and conversations is the impact it can have on our decision-making. Women are much more likely than men to come to conclusions and make decisions out of tangled hearts. Those conclusions, especially about God and his love for us, are often distorted by the confused and jumbled emotions that characterize the tangled heart.

How do our hearts get tangled?

First, we're women, and that means we have many emotions. From the time we enter puberty until long after menopause, emotions play an enormous part in our lives. A major factor in untangling our hearts involves the determination not to live by our emotions. If we don't control our emotions, they will most certainly control us. Of course we don't want to turn into emotionless robots, but neither do we want to be continually living at the mercy of our emotions. Our emotional nature as women is a huge part of the tangling process.

Second, we're alive, and that means we have experiences throughout our lives that are often entangling, especially if we cannot leave them behind us. No one comes through this life unscathed. Job 5:7: 'Yet man is born to trouble as surely as sparks fly upward.' Have you ever seen a fire where the sparks fly downward? We are born to trouble. The word translated 'trouble' in this verse means worry, whether of body or mind: grief, iniquity, labor, mischief, misery, pain, perverseness, sorrow, toil, travail, weariness, wickedness. These are the things we are born to, things we all experience. It is part of being human and living on a planet that 'groans' in the 'bondage to decay' (Rom. 8:20-22).

Third, we're human, and that means we are fallible. We make mistakes. We sin. And every mistake we make, every time we sin, every error in judgement and misstep we take has consequences. Every time we get it wrong, a tiny bit of the heart tangles, and after years of mistakes, those tiny bits join together into larger bits and intertwine with one another until the whole heart is tangled, knotted and bewildered. Even when we don't

17

make that many mistakes and don't get it wrong that often, we do not live in the Garden of Eden and our fallen human nature still plagues us. Job 14:1 says, 'Man born of woman is of few days and full of trouble.' Notice that it doesn't say 'unbelievers' or 'the ungodly'. It says man born of woman. What does that mean? Everyone. Life is full of trouble, even for those who belong to God through faith in Christ. We are to expect it.

Peter exhorted his dear friends to 'not be surprised at the painful trial you are suffering, as though something strange were happening to you' (1 Peter 4:12). Peter was speaking here to the believers in Jerusalem just before it was destroyed by the Romans in AD 70. The King James Version uses the phrase 'fiery trial' and Jerusalem was destroyed by fire. But the application to us is the same: we are to expect painful trials. They are not strange and we shouldn't be surprised that they are happening. 'No temptation has seized you except what is common to man' (1 Cor. 10:13). It is common for us to go through trials. It is part of being human.

Fourth, we're not alone on this planet. We're part of families, churches, communities and nations, all filled with fallible human beings. I heard someone say once that church would be great if it weren't for the people who go there. That's true of every group of people with which we involve ourselves. Our families are made up of fallible human beings whose hearts are bruised and battered by life, and whose days are full of trouble. Add to the mix several women in the same family, all dealing with sometimes out-of-control emotions, and it's a wonder anyone survives. When my daughter was going through her teenage years, I was just entering menopause (the result of incredibly bad timing on our part), and my poor husband often found himself in the middle of a 'cat fight'. More than once he must have felt as if he was choking on fur. Had I known then what I know now about the teen years and how to survive raising an emotionally sensitive girl, I would have been better equipped to handle it. Both our hearts became tangled through that experience, but we learn as we go in this life — another aspect of living among other fallible human beings.

Fifth, we're Christians, and that means a spiritual battle. We're going to look at this in depth in chapter three, but the tangling of Christian hearts often results from a lack of understanding that the Christian life is not hearts and flowers — it's a battle. And if we are not geared up for the battle, we are going to find ourselves lying wounded on the battlefield, unable to go any farther. Those who expect the journey to be easy and filled with happiness (which is vastly different from the joy we are promised in Christ) will be like Pliable, the character in *The Pilgrim's Progress* who turned back from the Way as soon as the going got tough, declaring: 'Is this the happiness you've been telling me about all this time?!' And with that, he turned back to the City of Destruction from where he had come.

Paul exhorts us to 'fight the good fight of the faith' (1 Tim. 6:12), to 'Put on the full armor of God' (Eph. 6:11), and to 'Endure hardship … like a good soldier of Christ Jesus' (2 Tim. 2:3). The war imagery in these verses should convince us that we are in a spiritual battle. If we fail to understand that truth, we are continually disappointed and confused by the difficulties we encounter, and doubts about God and the Christian life creep in and our hearts become tangled.

Fears and doubts

Women are especially susceptible to fears and doubts that tangle the heart, much more so than men, and we are more likely to act upon those fears and make decisions influenced by them. Here are some examples of women's fears and doubts and the reactions they produce.

1. *We fear illness and death*, both of ourselves and our loved ones. If fear gets the better of us, it can lead to irrational behavior regarding health and activities. Fearful mothers often won't let their children out of their sight. They become 'helicopter mothers' who hover over their children, watching their every move and dictating every decision. Of course we are to protect our children, but the fear that refuses to let them grow up, to make their own decisions as they mature, and yes, to suffer the consequences of their mistakes at the appropriate time, only ensures another generation of fearful parents and the cycle starts over again.

2. *We doubt that we are loved.* When a woman doubts that the man in her life really loves her, that doubt can lead to clinginess, possessiveness, suspiciousness. Oddly enough, that kind of behavior only lessens a man's love for a woman instead of increasing it. But the doubt can become so overwhelming that it impacts every word she utters and every action she performs toward her man. He begins to distance himself from her, which increases her doubt, and the whole thing becomes a downward spiral.

3. *We fear losing our attractiveness.* We all want to retain the charm and beauty we had when we were in our peak years, but

life has a way of sapping our vitality and taking the edge off the outward prettiness all women want to maintain. Every pound we gain, every gray hair and facial line that appears, reminds us of the loss of the person we once were. Fear of losing that and the rush to try to regain it can lead to an overemphasis on physical fitness, perpetual shopping for more and nicer clothes, and many hours in the hair salon and day spa.

4. *We have fears about children* — having them, not having them, what will happen to them and become of them. Childless women fear they may never be able to have children and their lives will be incomplete because of it. Women with children fear for their future, especially in a world that appears to be awash in cultural sewage that flows into our homes via TV, the Internet, and iPhones. We may doubt our ability to protect our kids or to ensure a secure future for them. Most of all, we doubt our ability to lead them to Christ and to live for him.

5. *We have doubts about our ability* to have successful relationships and, if we have them, that we can keep them. We fear being bad wives or mothers or daughters or friends. This can lead to isolating ourselves from other people, either physically or emotionally. We wall up our hearts in a prison of self-doubt and dare not venture out and offer ourselves to others. Or we offer ourselves guardedly and half-heartedly, fearing the rejection we are almost certain will come.

6. *We may doubt our worth* and fear what others will think of us. This can lead to pretending to be someone we're not, hiding our real selves and creating an alternate person that we show to others. This can result in living a life of lies, constantly adjusting our reactions to people and the way we express ourselves

to others. This kind of doubt can be exhausting mentally and emotionally, and can result in depression and confusion about our true identity.

7. *Women often fear doing the wrong thing*/making wrong decisions. This kind of anxiety can lead to inertia, doing nothing, and taking no responsibility in any area of life. There is nothing sadder than a woman who, from fear of making a mistake, has encouraged her husband to make all the decisions for decades, only to see her husband die before she does, leaving her completely helpless, unable to make the smallest decision, pay the bills, or even to provide for her own basic needs.

8. *We fear the aging process.* As women, we are especially susceptible to doubts about our ability to cope with the loss of youth and vitality that comes as a natural result of the aging process. We fear the loss of independence that comes with aging and the loneliness that often accompanies it. Depression in senior citizens is epidemic, especially in developed nations where we live longer and longer.

9. *There is the fear of natural disasters,* which are out of our control. Earthquakes, tornadoes, floods, hurricanes and tsunamis remind us of our utter vulnerability to the ravages of a creation that is in 'bondage to decay' (Rom. 8:21). Perhaps our utter helplessness to do anything about natural disasters is the most frightening thing about them. But maybe that is also the key to dealing with those fears. Knowing that our heavenly Father is ultimately in control of them and leaving them in his hands is the only way to alleviate those fears, assuming, of course, that we know him well enough to trust those hands.

10. Then *there are doubts about God*, our own salvation, and our worth in his eyes. It is nearly impossible to live a life of faith in a world that routinely rejects the truths of the Bible, calls God's goodness and mercy into question, and works overtime to convince us that either God doesn't exist or, if he does, that he isn't all that concerned with us. From the Garden of Eden, the enemy of our souls has been hard at work calling God's Word into question: 'Did God *really* say…?' (Gen. 3:1, emphasis added), and he is still at it. He also lives up to the name 'the accuser of the brothers' (Rev. 12:10) by planting those little niggling doubts in our minds: 'How could God love you? You're not good enough'; or 'You call yourself a Christian!? Look what you've done.'

These are the things that tangle our hearts. So the question is: how can hearts and minds and emotions be untangled? Or is it even possible? The answer to that question is an unequivocal *yes!* And I hope by the time you've finished reading this book, you are as confident of that as I am, not because I'm telling you so, but because God is telling you so. I cannot give you a 'quick fix' in these pages so that in a week or two you will be a strong, confident, fearless woman with an untangled heart. It doesn't work that way. This is a process, a lifelong process. But these five steps absolutely do work, and if you or those you counsel will apply them in the power of the Holy Spirit, you will find hearts untangling in an amazing way.

23

'Mrs Smith, we need to do an EKG'

Examining ourselves

Donna loved living in Colorado. Gone was the fear of sudden earthquakes that plagued her existence for over twenty years in California. The ground in Colorado felt so solid, and Donna's life was predictable and secure — until the blizzard hit. Although it was forecast days in advance, Donna's many activities hadn't included an update of the weather situation before she headed out that day. A snowstorm turns into a blizzard when the winds exceed 35 mph, with blowing and drifting snow that reduces visibility to less than ¼ mile, lasting three hours or more. This was a full-blown blizzard. As Donna drove toward her home on the outskirts of town, her heart began to pound. All she could see were the red brake lights of the car ahead of her, barely visible in the blinding snow, and soon even they disappeared. Blasts of wind would swamp the car and completely obscure the view momentarily as she drove blindly along what she thought was the road home. It wasn't.

In no time, Donna was hopelessly lost, having turned onto a road through a hay field that led to the vast open plains covering Eastern Colorado all the way to the Kansas border over a hundred miles away. Seeing her gas gauge at nearly empty, she stopped the car, opened her cell phone with shaking hands, and dialed her husband's number. He tried to calm his wife by telling her he had been watching the news coverage of the blizzard and knew that the military were using Humvees to rescue stranded motorists. But they could only rescue people if they could find them, and Donna had no idea where she was. She tried not to panic, but it was late in the day and the temperature was already well below freezing. She knew her gas wouldn't last long and when it ran out, so would the life-sustaining warmth in the car. Unknown to her, this storm was predicted to last at least twelve hours. Suddenly the battery on her cell phone beeped twice and her husband's voice was gone. At that moment, Donna understood the concept of being completely powerless. She was utterly incapable of doing anything to get herself out of this deadly predicament. She was lost, alone and helpless.

Trying to untangle our hearts by our own power and strength is exactly like Donna trying to save her own life at that moment — impossible. We have neither the resources nor the know-how to do so. For those who know Christ as Lord and Savior, however, all the power in the universe is at our disposal because the Holy Spirit, the *only* power source, resides in our hearts. The apostle Peter tells us to make our 'calling and election sure' (2 Peter 1:10). In other words, make sure you are truly a believer, that you truly belong to Christ. The advice that follows will only pertain to those who have the Holy Spirit, without whose presence in the heart and soul it is not possible to untangle the heart. Without his power, we are completely lost and helpless, just like Donna.

Donna's story had a happy ending that day. Using the signal from her cell phone, emergency teams located the cell tower situated only yards away from her car, and in no time she was transported to safety in an Army Humvee. When those strong, young soldiers lifted her from what could have been her tomb, she put herself willingly in their hands. But she never forgot the feeling of utter powerlessness that engulfed her that day. It is only when we place ourselves into the strong arms of God that we truly have power.

The only power source

Jesus said, 'Apart [i.e., separated] from me you can do nothing' (John 15:5). So the first step in untangling the heart is to have a reasonable assurance of the reality of your own salvation. Unless you are in Christ, you have no hope of untangling your heart. Why? Because when we are saved by faith in Christ, the Holy Spirit comes into our hearts, and his presence is absolutely essential to untangling our hearts. When we are in union with Christ, his Spirit produces the fruit we so desperately long for — love, joy, peace, patience, kindness and the rest of the fruit of the Spirit (Gal. 5:22-23). Anger, guilt, fear, bitterness, doubt and jealousy are fruits of the flesh. Those who don't have Christ, those who are not in him, have no power source because the Spirit does not live in their hearts, and they certainly cannot produce the fruit of the Spirit on their own.

But neither can those of us who are believers produce them on our own because they are not our fruit. They are the fruit *of the*

Spirit. We need to understand that. So how do we get the Spirit? Through Christ. We receive the Holy Spirit at the moment of salvation and he resides in our hearts from then on. There is just no hope of victory without the Spirit indwelling us.

Back in the 70s when evangelicalism was expanding rapidly, we were told never to doubt our salvation. You accepted Christ and that was the end of it. Never look back. Never doubt. It's a 'done deal'. If you prayed the prayer, walked the aisle, signed the card, threw a pine cone in the fire at camp, you were in! Never doubt it. But is that what the Bible says? No. It says, 'Examine yourselves to see whether you are in the faith; test yourselves. Do you not realize that Christ Jesus is in you — unless, of course, you fail the test?' (2 Cor. 13:5). So what is the test we have to pass? If Christ has saved us and the Spirit has come into our hearts, we should be able to see the evidence of that in our lives. That's the test. The Spirit doesn't come into the heart of a person at salvation then sit there doing nothing for the rest of her life. He *will* produce fruit. We should see the fruit that comes from abiding in the Vine, which is Christ. To have any hope of untangling our hearts, it is crucial that we examine ourselves to see whether we are truly Christians.

Marks of a Christian

Let us look at a passage that describes a Christian, 2 Peter 1:1-8 (NKJV): 'Simon Peter, a bondservant and apostle of Jesus Christ, to those who have obtained like precious faith with us by the righteousness of our God and Savior Jesus Christ: Grace and peace be multiplied to you in the knowledge of God and of Jesus our Lord, as His divine power has given to us all things that pertain to life and godliness, through the knowledge of Him

27

who called us by glory and virtue, by which have been given to us exceedingly great and precious promises, that through these you may be partakers of the divine nature, having escaped the corruption that is in the world through lust. But also for this very reason, giving all diligence, add to your faith virtue, to virtue knowledge, to knowledge self-control, to self-control perseverance, to perseverance godliness, to godliness brotherly kindness, and to brotherly kindness love. For if these things are yours and abound, you will be neither barren nor unfruitful in the knowledge of our Lord Jesus Christ.'

These are the marks of a Christian. Not all Christians will exhibit all these traits all the time, but we should be growing and maturing in them, not because we are working hard at showing them, but because we have been given his divine power in 'all things that pertain to life and godliness' (v. 3). We have the power of the Holy Spirit within us. Peter lists the things that characterize a Christian, and then he tells us to 'make our calling and election sure'. How do we do that? By looking honestly at ourselves to see whether these things are in our lives.

Have you escaped, or are you in the process of escaping, the corruption that is in the world? Or are you still drawn to it through the lust of the eyes, the lust of the flesh and the pride of life? Do you spend more time on Facebook than in the Scriptures? Are you fascinated by the sordid lives of Hollywood personalities, knowing more about the lives of rock stars and Hollywood actresses than you do about the life of Jesus? Do you rush out to buy every new gadget that comes on the market? Is your closet a revolving door of new clothes and shoes? If you answered 'yes' to any of these questions, you may not really have escaped the corruption that is in the world.

28

Another translation of 'the pride of life' reads 'the pride of the age', and every age has some peculiarities in which pride reveals itself. In our age, it's what causes us to secretly exult when the rich and famous are arrested or get divorced. The natural man gloats over someone else's misfortunes, especially if we perceive they are living the high life. When they fall, it elevates our pride. Pride in our age can be material, striving after success, political power, or the achievements of our children. It's part of the battle against the flesh that we all have to wage. All these things are not of the Father but of the world which is in the control of Satan.

You know you have been saved by faith, but are you adding virtue (goodness) to that faith? Are you pursuing knowledge? Do you exhibit self-control? Do you persevere in the things of God? Do you exhibit godliness in your life? (The word translated 'godliness' literally means patience.) Are you patient? Are you kind to others? Then there's love. This is the word *agape*, which is the kind of love God has for us which caused him to go to the cross. Not sloppy sentimentality, but sacrificial love. Do you love others sacrificially? Even when you don't feel gushy and 'gooey' about them? Do you think God saved us because he felt all gushy about us? That we were so lovable that we deserved to be loved? No. He chose to love us and sacrifice himself for us in spite of ourselves as a deliberate act of his will for his name's sake and his glory. Do we choose to love others in spite of themselves, as a deliberate act of the will in order to give God the glory?

We all need to examine ourselves to see if we are truly in the faith. If you doubt that you are saved, I cannot give you assurance, and neither can your pastor, your husband, or your friends. Only God can do that, so ask him to reveal the eternal state of your soul to you. God has promised that 'The Spirit himself testifies with our spirit that we are God's children' (Rom. 8:16). The woman who has doubts as to the state of her soul has only to ask the Spirit for confirmation that she belongs to him. He will respond because he has promised to do so. If you are still unsure about your eternal standing before God, ask! If you want to have assurance of salvation, ask! And keep on asking until you get an answer. Jesus promised that if we ask and seek and knock, we will receive an answer. So ask! Pray a prayer similar to this: 'Lord, you promised that your Spirit would testify (corroborate, give evidence) that I belong to you. Please do that for me! Please give me the assurance deep in my heart that I am truly your child.' As with all God's promises to his children, he will do as he promised because he is trustworthy and faithful.

Make no mistake about it — self-deception is common. There are tares among the wheat, millions of pew-sitters who want to believe they are saved because of some past act or family tradition, who never look closely at their lives to see if it's real. We all have to do that — regularly. There is no other salvation except Christ, and the consequences of misjudging our spiritual state are ghastly. I don't want anyone reading this book to have to hear the terrible words from the Lord, '...I never knew you. Away from me...' (Matt. 7:23).

So examine yourselves and tell those you counsel to do the same as a first step in your counseling, because — and this is very important — no amount of advice or counseling will solve your problems if your biggest problem is that you are separated from God. That is why this has to be the first step in untangling hearts. But once salvation is reasonably assured, you can begin the process of moving forward with the understanding that you are not alone, that you do have the power of the Holy Spirit, and that you 'may participate in the divine nature' as Peter promised in 2 Peter 1:4. Think of that! Do you think of yourself as a partner or a participant in the nature of God? Not in the sense of being 'little gods' ourselves, but by being 'in Christ', he is in us and at work in us. Our new nature is his nature, of which we are part, and in that new nature, we are 'more than conquerors through him who loved us' (Rom. 8:37). Without that new nature, we are hopelessly lost and powerless — just like Donna.

The presence of the Holy Spirit in us is much more than an emotional jolt every Sunday morning that causes us to raise our hands and weep. The Spirit opens our minds and hearts to truths that are unknown and incomprehensible to those without the Spirit. All of life, all of life's problems and battles, all of life's trials and victories, are at their very core spiritual. As Christians, we have the ability to understand that because we are guided by the Holy Spirit who teaches us 'all things', who enlightens our eyes, and who leads us 'into all truth' (John 16:13). He is the one who enables us to see beneath the surface of the causes of the tangled heart, so that we say, 'Aha! I know what's going on.' Those without the Holy Spirit are easily overwhelmed by circumstances because they have no ability to see the spiritual forces at work behind them. 'The natural man does not receive the things of the Spirit of God, for they are foolishness to him; nor can he know them, because they are spiritually discerned' (1 Cor. 2:14).

What are the Spirit-revealed truths about life?

For one thing, we understand the reason that women are prone to tangled hearts in the first place. It all began in the Garden of

Eden and the fall of mankind into sin. Our sinful nature, which we inherited from Adam (Rom. 5:12), affects us in everything we do. It colors our perspectives, it causes us to do and think and feel things we don't really want to do and think and feel, and it wages war within us. But as Christians, we recognize the spiritual aspect of the tangled heart in a way that those without Christ cannot see.

As women with the Holy Spirit, we understand that part of the sin nature affecting us has to do with our hormones. The whole mess that involves our hormones comes from the sin of Eve. God said, 'I will greatly increase your pains in childbearing; with pain you will give birth to children' (Gen. 3:16). I am convinced that part of the curse on women is the pain we bear, not only giving birth to children, but also the emotional pain that results from the hormones associated with childbirth. If it were merely labor pains, then single and childless women would be exempt from the curse; so it has to be more than that. The hormones linked with being a woman and the misery they cause are part of the curse that is common to womanhood and the part that helps to tangle our hearts.

As women who understand the reality of the Fall, we can also understand the enormity of the precious gift of the Savior, Jesus Christ, who came to save us from our sin natures and create in us new life. We take comfort in the Spirit who lives within us, knowing that the victory ultimately belongs to him. Sadly, those without the Spirit are at the mercy of their hormones and the sin nature that controls them, and untangling their hearts in a meaningful way is just as impossible for them as it was for Donna to save herself from the blizzard.

As Christian women, we have the precious gift of God's Word to guide us, enlighten us and assure us in ways that others do not. We know the 'beginning from the end' and we know who is in charge of it all. We look to the future with hope and are not overwhelmed with despair as we see the culture imploding around us. We have what those who are not in Christ cannot have — the wisdom that 'comes from heaven' (James 3:17), wisdom that God grants to his children when they ask for it (James 1:5), and by that wisdom we know that there are events taking place 'behind the scenes' as spiritual forces battle for the hearts and minds of people.

The Bible also assures us that no matter how bleak our circumstances, God will never bring a trial into our lives so great as to overwhelm us completely. Paul assures us that 'No temptation has seized you except what is common to man. And God is faithful; he will not let you be tempted beyond what you can bear. But when you are tempted, he will also provide a way out so that you can stand up under it' (1 Cor. 10:13). God knows your breaking point and he won't let it go past that point. Life throws numerous trials at us — illness, cancer, accidents, financial hardships, death. Each trial makes us stronger and better able to handle the next one. The trial of the tangled heart, like all others, is designed to show you that your faith is real. In Christ, we can face the trials of life with grace, good humor and complete faith that whatever God has for us is ok. But this doesn't happen overnight. This comes from years of walking with him, trial upon trial upon trial.

As Christian women, we understand the reality of the presence of God in our lives if we truly belong to him. His nature, his character and attributes are revealed to us by his Spirit who gives us the assurance of his love and care for us. We know he isn't going to let us be defeated by our circumstances. Even when you don't think you can bear it any longer, you haven't reached the end of your rope because God has promised not to let you get there. If you belong to him, you can depend on his faithfulness. When the pressure becomes too much to bear, he is faithful to throw you a life preserver and pull you to shore. This is just one of the ways he will prove himself faithful in your life.

He also promises that in each trial, he will 'provide a way out'. But the way out does not include being taken out of the trial. You're in the trial for a purpose. The way out is the way *through*. God doesn't pull us out from under the trial. Why would he if he says the trial is for our benefit? Rather, the way out is him seeing us through it to the other side. Think of it as being in a huge maze with ten-foot hedges on either side of narrow paths. God is not going to swoop in like a helicopter and pluck you out of the maze. But he's going to walk by your side and guide you through it and show you the way out. Along the way, you'll be weary and heart sore, but he'll be with you all the way, sometimes leading, sometimes pushing, sometimes letting you lean on him, sometimes carrying you, all the way to the exit of the maze. Once through the maze, there is a sunny green meadow with beautiful flowers, birds singing and a gentle breeze. But guess what is on the far side of the meadow? Another maze. But for the woman with Christ and the Spirit residing in her, each maze, each trial, strengthens, encourages and ultimately places in her strong, settled convictions of the reality of her salvation. This is so encouraging to those who struggle — knowing we're not alone in our struggles and that the power of God himself is available to us because he promised it!

We can read it, we can say we believe it, but in our day-to-day lives, we don't act like we believe it. Why? Often because we don't really understand that the Christian life is a battle. We think that we should have victory over sin, instant relief from the things that plague us — the doubts, fears, anxieties, anger, bitterness, depression. And when those victories don't come, or we do have victory over them and then they come back again, we sink under the weight of disappointment because what we thought was going to happen — the victory — either doesn't come or doesn't stay. This takes us to the second part of the untangling process.

3

'Don't you know there's a war on?'

The Christian life is a battle, so gear up

There is a scene at the beginning of the beloved Christmas classic *It's a Wonderful Life* in which Clarence Oddbody, AS2 (Angel, Second Class) is shown events in the life of his charge, George Bailey. Because of his 'bad ear' George can't enlist in World War II, staying home instead to 'fight the battle of Bedford Falls'. In one of the scenes of George performing his duties, he reminds people that they cannot expect things to be the same as they used to be, and he challenges them with the famous line, 'Don't you know there's a war on?!'

'Don't you know there's a war on?' is a question well known to the WWII generation. My mother, who lived through that conflict, was so ingrained with the idea of necessary sacrifices and life changes due to the war that, for long after it was over, she continued to use that expression. When we would leave lights on in empty rooms, she would bellow, 'Turn off the lights! Don't you know there's a war on?!' When we wasted food or left the water running in the sink, she would ask if we didn't know that there was a war on. We got so used to this little scene that my brothers and I reached the point of saying, 'We know, Mom, there's a war on', before she had the chance to get on her soap box. The fact that, at that time, the country was not at war didn't deter her. 'Don't you know there's a war on?' had become the standard rallying cry to change behavior, to sacrifice in some way, to be in a defensive mode, or to live prepared for some kind of conflict.

The WWII generation knew what war was all about. Even though it was being fought in Europe, the 'home front' was part of the battle. They lived it day in and day out for years, and every part of their lives was involved in the war effort. Everything they did was affected by the war that threatened their way of life. Preparation on the home front included sacrifices which were gladly embraced because they understood that the threat was real. At home, posters shouted slogans to motivate citizens to guard their speech ('Loose lips sink ships!'), to take action ('Uncle Sam wants YOU!'; 'Buy war bonds!'), or to change their behavior in the face of the grave threat ('Make do and mend'; and yes, even 'Put that light OUT!').

That generation knew some things about war against Nazism that Christians must recognize about the spiritual war we wage if we are to untangle our hearts. They knew who the enemy was and how to defeat him, and they knew they were in it for the long haul. War against the enemy of our souls is real, the enemy is powerful and relentless, we must be totally engaged in the battle, and changes in our thinking and our actions are necessary to defeat him.

Against what/whom do we battle?

When Paul told the Christians in the church at Ephesus to 'put on the full armor of God' (Eph. 6:11-18), he wasn't referring to physical armor. Our struggle is 'not against flesh and blood', meaning that it is not people we are at war with, although it certainly seems that way at times. When others come against us in the spiritual battle, we have to recognize that they are mere pawns, moved by the hand of their general, Satan. They are essentially his puppets, and he pulls their strings and directs them against the people of God. Because they have no power to resist him, they are instruments of 'the powers of this dark world' and 'the spiritual forces of evil in the heavenly realms' (Eph. 6:12).

There is no doubt that those powers and forces are Satan and his demonic hosts who preside over the ignorance, sin, misery and darkness that characterize the unbelieving world. Never mistake the caricature of Satan — an imp in a red suit with a pitchfork — for the powerful enemy of our souls. Rather, he is ruthless, cunning and relentless, and he controls a vast empire of foul and malignant spirits who wage war against God and his people. No empire has been so extended, or has continued so long, as that empire of darkness, and nothing on earth is so difficult to destroy. But it was this very empire that the Redeemer came to vanquish, and it is only by his power that we are enabled to stand our ground against it.

The battle against the forces of darkness is fought upon the same battlefields as Christians have inhabited since the beginning of time. They are the battlefields of our own sinful flesh and the evil passions of others — their pride, ambition and spirit of revenge.

The battlefields are also the evil customs, laws, opinions, politics and pleasures of the world, as well as the error, superstition and false doctrines which are part of that kingdom. Wherever we come in contact with evil is the battlefield in the spiritual war. But again, this is not a war fought with physical weapons. We do not flog ourselves with whips; we don't use our tongues to blister those under the control of demonic forces; we don't blow up our enemies or cut off their heads. We do not fight evil with evil. Rather, we put on the 'full armor of God' in order to withstand the 'flaming arrows' of the enemy. Our weapons are truth, righteousness, the gospel of peace, faith, prayer and the sword of the Spirit which is the Word of God. Against these, Satan is powerless, and victory against him is assured.

How does he fight?

We have to understand that Satan does not carry on an open warfare. He does not meet the Christian face to face. His is a covert war. He makes his approaches when he perceives we are at our most vulnerable, and he seeks to confuse and delude us rather than to vanquish by mere force, which is why our spiritual armor must be kept polished. A soldier who has to contend with a visible enemy may feel safe as he prepares to meet him in the open field. But it is completely different if the enemy is invisible, one who steals up slyly and stealthily. Such is the foe that we have to contend with. The Christian life is a struggle against a wily enemy. Satan does not openly appear in a repulsive form, but comes disguised as an angel of light (2 Cor. 11:14) to recommend some plausible lie, to present to us some temptation that might seem alluring and satisfying. Recognizing the enemy and his battle plan is crucial to untangling hearts.

One of the effective ways Satan attacks us is through the culture. Those who like to say that 'Satan is doing this, that and the other thing' to them are operating on the false assumption that Satan is targeting them personally. Satan is not an omnipresent being as God is. He is a created being and, as such, he can only be in one place at a time. But he has hordes of demonic forces and he spreads his influence throughout the culture we live in, infecting every aspect of it with his deceit and lies. 'We know that we are children of God, and that the whole world is under the control of the evil one' (1 John 5:19). This means that every institution and every level of society is influenced by Satan — government, education, entertainment, technology, yes, even religion to a great extent. Isn't that obvious every time we turn on the news or surf the internet?

Satan's lies and manipulations come primarily through the culture that invades our lives through every avenue of media. Remember that Satan's method of deceit always follows the same three temptations, the same three lies he purveyed in the Garden as described in Genesis 3:1-6. Eve entertained the serpent's lies, then saw that the fruit was 'good for food' (lust of the flesh), 'pleasing to the eye' (lust of the eyes), and 'desirable for gaining wisdom' (the pride of life). These three things are the basis of what the world offers and markets. It is all lies.

The truth is that when we succumb to the lust of the flesh, the lust of the eyes and the pride of life, whatever we get, whatever we do, it's never enough. That's the secret to resisting the lies of the culture. All marketing is based on the same premise: 'Buy this! It will make you ____ (fill in the blank with whatever it is you want)!' No, it won't. It's just another lie designed to feed our dissatisfaction and play on our fears and insecurities and our desire for more 'stuff'. Marketing is designed to create the gross national appetite for the gross national product. In reality, nothing we can buy will satisfy us. Don't believe the culture's lies. Be satisfied with Christ because he's the only One who *can* satisfy you.

What are our weapons?

Imagine for a moment that you were drafted into the armed forces and sent to a foreign land to fight a vicious and well-armed military. Would you consider trotting out onto the battlefield in the middle of a ferocious fire fight wearing a tank top with spaghetti straps, hip-hugger shorts that bared your midriff, flip-flops and a baseball cap, and carrying nothing but your cell phone and iPod? How long do you think you would last on that battlefield? Isn't that a ridiculous image? Yet, when we try to wage spiritual warfare against Satan and his foul fiends without the armor that God provides, that's exactly what we do.

The full armor of God contains defensive weapons that are mighty and powerful, (and) the way we think about them influences how we perceive that power. We are to put around our waists the belt of truth, imagining not a simple string belt worn for decoration, but a thick leather belt covered with metal studs. Truth is a strong protector of our inner selves, the part our belts cover. The 'breastplate of righteousness' is not a skimpy garment but a coat of metal that covers our most vulnerable parts, including the heart and lungs. The breastplate of a soldier covered his most vital body parts, and the idea here is that the moral righteousness of Christian character is as necessary to defend us from the assaults of Satan as the coat of armor was to preserve the heart of a Roman soldier from the arrows of an enemy.

Further, our feet are to be covered with 'the readiness of the gospel of peace'. No one walks through the mud and filth of the battlefield in sandals. Like the boots worn by soldiers to carry them safely through many obstructions and snares of the battlefield, our feet must be prepared to walk through any trial, any opposition and still remain a solid foundation upon which we can stand. We don't use our boots to stomp those who oppose us, however, but we are ready to peaceably present the gospel, always ready to give an answer for the hope that is within us, with gentleness and respect (1 Peter 3:15).

We hold before us the 'shield of faith', which is not like the papier-mâché shields our children make in preschool. Obviously they would be worthless against the fiery arrows the enemy throws at us. The Roman soldier's shield was an ingenious device by which blows and arrows might be repelled and the whole body defended. It could be held up to protect the head, lowered to protect the legs, or thrown behind to meet attacks from the rear. As long as the soldier had his shield, he felt secure, and as long as a Christian has faith, she is able to repel the attacks of the enemy.

The helmet of salvation is that which protects the mind and the thoughts. The image here is not of a baseball cap or a sun visor, but a heavy bronze or steel covering for the entire head, with a visor that can be lowered to cover the face. A well-founded hope of salvation will preserve us in the day of spiritual conflict, and will guard us from the blows which an enemy would strike at our minds. Those blows take the form of doubts he plants in our minds about our position in Christ, about God's love for

We must KNOW our identity in Christ.

us, about our usefulness to God, and about our eternal destiny. The helmet of salvation protects our heads, our minds, and our thoughts from those doubts and insecurities as surely as a bronze helmet protected a soldier from the blows of his enemy.

The full armor of God which we are to put on includes only one offensive weapon, the 'sword of the Spirit, which is the word of God'. We parry and thrust with that sword, the timeless truths of the Bible, hacking and slicing at the lies of the enemy, lies which abound in all aspects of modern culture. But that is the *only* offensive action we are to take. We put on our armor, take up the sword and 'stand'. Paul exhorts us to 'put on the full armor of God so that you can *take your stand* against the devil's schemes' (Eph. 6:11, emphasis added). He goes on to say, 'Therefore put on the full armor of God, so that when the day of evil comes, you may be able to *stand your ground*, and after you have done everything, *to stand*' (v. 13, emphasis added).

The repeated use of the word 'stand' is significant. Nothing in these verses commands us to chase after Satan or attempt to cast out demons. Nowhere in the New Testament is a believer *ever* commanded to cast out demons as part of the Christian life. Jesus and the disciples cast out demons only to demonstrate to others that their authority and power was from God. Now that we have the completed Word of God, casting out demons is no longer necessary or commanded. The epistles (Romans through Jude) refer to demonic activity, yet do not describe casting them out, nor are believers ever exhorted to do so or told that we should even consider doing so.

We use the armor to deflect the enemy's blows, to ward off the lies and evil he brings against us, in order to stand our ground, firmly resisting him, which we know is the way to cause him to leave us alone. James 4:7 tells us to 'resist the devil' and he will flee from us. We are not to enter into his realm to do battle with him. We are simply not strong enough for that. Even Michael, the mighty archangel of God, did not battle Satan, saying instead, 'The Lord rebuke you!' (Jude 1:9). But God has given us sufficient defensive armor to withstand him, and we stand firmly in the confidence that God's power alone will eventually defeat him for ever.

Overshadowing every battle is the weapon of prayer, as Paul says in Ephesians 6:18. After describing all the pieces of the armor, he ends with, 'And pray in the Spirit on all occasions with all kinds of prayers and requests. With this in mind, be alert and always keep on praying for all the saints.' Praying 'in the Spirit' isn't some kind of mystical, experiential prayer that requires us to feel a certain way before we pray. It simply means praying in a manner consistent with who God is and in accordance with his will. Our effective weapon of prayer is that which lines up with God's will and glorifies him. And the only way to be sure our prayers line up with his will is to know his perfect will, and that is only revealed in the Bible.

Paul also encourages us to pray continually, on all occasions, with all kinds of prayers offered both for ourselves and others. How comforting to know that other saints (believers) are struggling in the same spiritual battle, holding up their own shields of faith and resisting the forces of darkness. They need our prayers just as we need theirs, a perfect picture of the body of Christ laboring side by side against the lies and 'flaming arrows' of the evil one.

How long does the battle last?

One of the changes to our thinking that must occur if we are to have any hope of untangling our hearts is the recognition that we are in a lifelong battle, whether we like it or not. Unlike the WWII generation, we can't expect the end of the war to come in a year or two or five. The Christian life begins the moment we come to Christ in faith and continues until the day we die. Hard as it is to accept, this is a lifelong battle. As much as I would like to give you a few 'steps to victory' which will transform your life overnight, that simply isn't possible.

Paul told Timothy to 'Endure hardship … like a good soldier of Christ Jesus. No one serving as a soldier gets involved with civilian affairs — he wants to please his commanding officer' (2 Tim. 2:3-4). 'Enduring' means going on in continuous warfare. The battlefields will change as we grow and mature. We battle different things, but the war never ends. Not in this life. And if we think it does, that false idea tangles our hearts because we expect something we're not going to get.

We have to get past the idea of total victory in the war we wage here and now. There are small victories but the war rages on. Sometimes we think that if we could just get to that level of spiritual maturity where we can have victory over sin, have no more spiritual battles within, then we could really do something for God, really be a help to others because we are no longer fighting the battles. But the closer you get to God and the more you are involved in ministry, the more intense the battle becomes, because the enemy is working harder to stop you. You're on the front lines and he's throwing everything he has at you. You're more of a threat to his kingdom and he's making it harder than ever to keep going.

Paul was mature in the faith, wasn't he? He was the chief of the Apostles commissioned by Jesus himself to preach to the Gentiles. Did he have it easy? 'Five times I received from the Jews the forty lashes minus one. Three times I was beaten with rods, once I was stoned, three times I was shipwrecked, spent a night and a day in the open sea, I have been constantly on the move. I have been in danger from rivers, in danger from bandits, in danger from my own countrymen, in danger from Gentiles; in danger in the city, in danger in the country, in danger at sea; and in danger from false brothers. I have labored and toiled and have often gone without sleep; I have known hunger and thirst and have often gone without food; I have been cold and naked. Besides everything else, I face daily the pressure of my concern for all the churches' (2 Cor. 11:24-28).

Wow. You wouldn't want to use Paul as a marketing tool to get people to sign up for the faith! Could God have kept him from experiencing all these things? Sure. Did he? No. Why? So that Paul would grow and mature in his faith and would write down his experiences for us to read and be encouraged that we are not the only ones, or the first ones, to experience these things. *Well, Paul didn't have to deal with a husband who isn't a spiritual leader or children who are Facebook junkies or teenagers! Paul never had to deal with PMS!* Look. Satan and his demons are working overtime to win the victory over you, crush your spirit, and get you out of the game. The enemy's intent is to shipwreck your faith, and if he can use your husband or your kids or your hormones to do it, he will. 1 Peter 5:8 says, 'Be self-controlled and alert. Your enemy the devil prowls around like a roaring lion looking for someone to devour.' We have to 'be alert' — recognize and understand that. He knows where we are weak and will use it against us. But take heart. As we battle throughout our lives, we do so with the understanding that the hope before us is heaven, a world that knows no sin and no more battling. It's not about the here and now; it's about the then and there.

But I want my life to be great now! Doesn't God want me to be happy? God never promises happiness in this life. It's in the next life where we will receive 'an inheritance that can never perish, spoil or fade — kept in heaven for you' (1 Peter 1:4). How can any life now compare with an eternity in God's presence, face to face with Jesus? Life here and now is trouble, persecution and sorrow. Learning to view the Christian life in terms of a battle in the spiritual war is essential to remaining in the battle, not being defeated by the enemy, and coming out of it better people for it. So put on the full armor of God, fight the good fight, and don't give up or give in.

How do our hearts get tangled up because of the battle?

Satan continually tries to influence us to give in to the flesh, and he wins the war when he can get us to sink in despair so that we give up the daily fight. Many Christians lose the battle daily by listening to him as he tangles up our hearts by manipulating our thoughts and emotions, instead of listening to God and living by faith. Demonic forces constantly feed our fears and doubts because they know that will weaken our faith. They don't have to work on us personally; the culture they control constantly does their dirty work for them.

We have to remember that Satan is 'a liar and the father of lies' (John 8:44). He began to influence women in the Garden of Eden when he lied in his subtle way to Eve, causing her to doubt God's words ('Did God *really* say…?'), then by directly contradicting God ('You will not surely die'). Then he called God's motives into question by telling her that God didn't want any competition (Gen. 3:5). Of course these were lies. All of Satan's lies have as their goal the destruction of God's character and nature in our eyes.

All our doubts about God come from Satan's lies. When we think, *God can't possibly love me because…*, we are listening to the lies of Satan. We will talk more about the doubts he causes in a later chapter, but if you doubt God's love, mercy, grace and patience, you are listening to the devil's lies. If you doubt that you can be of use in his kingdom, you are listening to Satan's lies. If you doubt what God has revealed in his Word and fall for the false doctrines of cults or quasi-Christian religions, you are listening to Satan's lies. If you doubt that you can be happy without the 'stuff' of a materialistic culture, you are listening to Satan's lies. So buckle that belt of truth tightly around you so you can tell the difference between the truth of God and the lies of the devil.

Suppose I don't want to fight?

No one likes to fight. Even soldiers who volunteer to go into battle in foreign lands only do so to secure peace for their families and their country. What would happen if not a single young man or woman had volunteered to fight Hitler in WWII and those who were drafted simply refused to go? Evil would have won the day and Hitler would have ruled the world. While it might seem appealing to sit back and leave it to the pastor and church leaders to fight the spiritual battle, we must understand the dire consequences of refusing to enter the fray.

I was once asked by a Christian woman who had struggled in a bad marriage for years whether it wouldn't be better to just throw in the towel. She and her Christian husband had simply decided to give up and 'give Satan the victory this time'. If you've ever felt that way, you must never think that giving Satan a victory is a viable alternative to fighting him with all that is within you. We know that he is our 'enemy the devil [who] prowls around like a roaring lion looking for someone to devour' (1 Peter 5:8). His desire to devour you will never be satisfied by a single victory over you. His appetite for your soul is as ravenous as a wolf's and if you give him one victory, he will be back for more, and your ability to resist him in the future will be seriously compromised. In fact, once he has a taste for victory in your life, his efforts against you will be doubled because your resistance to him will have been seriously weakened. Giving up and giving in to Satan is never an option.

Another reason we cannot pull ourselves out of the battle is that we displease the Lord by doing so. He has commanded us to 'fight the good fight of the faith' (1 Tim. 6:12) and that involves buckling on the armor and picking up the shield and sword, not hiding in the foxholes of our lives. How can we expect God's blessings and be unwilling to endure the hardship of the battle for him? How can we think about him dying on the cross to snatch us out of the devil's grip and be so ungrateful for that sacrifice as to doubt his power to see us through the battle to victory? And how can we expect to win a lost world for Christ if we are not in the battle for their souls? And what about our own children? What message do we send them about God's ability to sustain them through the battles that will surely come in their own lives? No. Giving up and sitting on the sidelines of the battlefield is not the Christian life. By being in the war, we make our calling and election sure. You can always tell the dead fish from the live ones in a stream. The dead fish float along with the current on top of the water. The live fish are deep in the water battling with every bit of their strength against the current. Don't be a dead fish! We *are* soldiers of the cross, so we have to put on our armor and get into the battle. *Don't you know there's a war on?!*

So the first two principles for untangling hearts are to be sure we are truly in the faith and then to recognize that the Christian life is a battle. One of the biggest battles we fight as women is our emotions. The greatest battle is the internal one, the battle of the heart, the seat of our emotions. And so often negative emotions are nothing more than lies that the enemy uses to stop us in our tracks, turn our thoughts inward, and derail us from the battle. So the third principle for untangling our hearts is that we are not to live by our emotions. In the next few chapters, we're going to do some soul-searching about the negative emotions that we have to fight day in and day out — fear, doubt, guilt, anger, bitterness, envy and jealousy. All these are battlegrounds where the daily battles of the Christian life, especially for women, are fought.

4

Where is Robocop when you need him?

Women's emotions and how they affect us

Imagine for a moment that you are standing on the hill at Golgotha 2000 years ago and you see before you three crosses. On one of them hangs the Savior, Jesus Christ, about to be crucified for the sins of the world. Then imagine that he looks around and suddenly hops off the cross saying, 'You know, I just don't feel like doing this.' Then he walks off into the sunset. Unimaginable? Yes. But this is what the modern Christian does every time she allows her feelings to dictate her actions or her thought processes.

Contemporary Western culture is a culture based on feelings. We are told, 'If it feels good, do it', and the unspoken corollary is that if it doesn't feel good, we won't (and shouldn't have to) do it. Unfortunately, this secular philosophy has seeped into the Evangelical church, where our every whim and desire is catered for, and where services and programs are based on the felt needs and wants of those in the pews. Sadly, many are deceived by this paradigm, believing that their feelings are the most important thing in life, although that idea is entirely antithetical to the teachings of Scripture.

The Bible is filled with godly men and women doing God's will in obedience, regardless of their feelings at the time. Surely Abraham didn't feel like sacrificing his only son on the altar, but he was willing to do it because God had directed him to do so (Gen. 22). Similarly, the apostle Paul describes what he suffered in order to bring the gospel to the Gentiles: beatings, stonings, shipwrecks, hunger, thirst, sleeplessness, cold and constant danger (2 Cor. 11). Can we suppose he went through these things because he felt like it? Of course Jesus didn't 'feel like' going to the cross to bear the burden of our sin, but he did it, motivated by the same thing that motivated Abraham and Paul: love for and obedience to God. They all knew something we have lost track of in modern life — our feelings must not dictate our thoughts and actions.

Feelings versus truth

The third of the five principles for freeing tangled hearts is: '*Don't live by your feelings.*' Notice I didn't say, 'Don't *have* feelings.' I said don't *live by* your feelings. God has emotions — love, hate, jealousy, anger, sorrow, joy. Our emotional nature is a reflection of being made in his image. But that image is corrupted by sin which affects every part of us, and, as women, it especially affects our emotions. But emotions are untrustworthy. Feelings are not reliable. They ebb and flow like the tides of the sea that bring in all kinds of seaweed and debris, and deposit them on the shore then go back out, eroding the ground we stand on and washing it out to sea. Such is the state of those whose emotions rule their lives. The simplest circumstances — a headache, a cloudy day, a word thoughtlessly spoken by a friend or a family member — can erode our confidence and send us 'out to sea' in a fit of despair. How much more the really difficult circumstances of life!

James 1:6

To have any hope of freeing our tangled hearts, we simply must distinguish between what our emotions are telling us and what God's Word is telling us. But emotions are so powerful, so persuasive, and so personal that we listen to them more often than we listen to God. I once received an e-mail from a woman named Jessie who described her feelings and the way they influenced her thoughts and behavior: '*I feel that I have sinned so much that maybe God thinks that I am so sinful that I should not be forgiven. Seems like others feel God's spirit and are blessed but me, I pray and I feel like God does not hear me. What do you do when you don't hear what God is saying and what he is trying to let you know? Help. (signed) unhappy.*'

Here is a perfect example of a tangled heart caused by feelings which override truth about God and cause wrong conclusions about him. Jessie was projecting her own feelings about herself onto God and assuming he is thinking about her in the way she thinks about herself. She doesn't understand the forgiveness of sin and that 'there is now no condemnation for those who are in Christ Jesus' (Rom. 8:1). It's not that God thinks she's so sinful she can't be forgiven, because his Word says otherwise. Rather, she *feels* that she is too sinful to be forgiven. She prays, but *feels* like God doesn't hear her, in spite of the fact that he is always 'close to the brokenhearted' (Ps. 34:18) and has promised to hear all who call upon him. She has already rejected what he said about forgiveness and yet she wants to hear more from him. Of course she's unhappy. Listening to our own thoughts and drawing conclusions from our feelings, which are so easily influenced by outside forces, is a sure way to unhappiness.

But the Christian woman who is forewarned and well armed is a woman not governed by circumstances, but by the truth she knows, and one whose emotions are derived from truth, instead of the other way round. She does not ask herself: *'Why don't I feel saved?'* or *'Why do other people have joy in their worship while I don't?'* or *'Can God really be there if I don't feel his presence?'* or *'Why am I always depressed/anxious/doubtful?'* This is precisely the error many women make. They respond to their feelings and turn in upon themselves, becoming preoccupied with themselves, constantly analyzing their own feelings and, by extension, their attitudes, problems, relationships and circumstances. Our feelings are not the issue. Truth is the issue. God's truth. When we experience positive emotions based on truth, that's a joyful thing. When we experience negative emotions not based on God's truth, our hearts become tangled.

That is not to say we need to get rid of our emotions. Emotions make us who we are — human and female. We don't want to become emotionless robots. We want to feel and feel deeply. We want to experience love and compassion and emotional highs. What we don't want to do is to *live by* our feelings. The goal is to manage our emotions instead of letting them manage us; to recognize when they are lying to us and when Satan is using them to deceive us; to know what to do with negative emotions like fear, doubt, anger, guilt, bitterness and envy in order to keep them from ruling our lives and tangling our hearts; and to be able to experience fewer and fewer negative emotions as we mature and experience more and more of the positive emotions — peace, joy, contentment, love and hope. Isn't that what we all want?

How our emotions affect our thinking

Emotions originate in the heart, but they affect the mind and the body. Depression causes fatigue. Fear knots up the stomach and causes digestive problems. Anger produces tension in the neck and shoulders. Doubt knits the brow. But most importantly, negative emotions tangle our hearts because they affect our minds and cause cloudy, confused thinking. Worst of all, they cause us to come to wrong conclusions about ourselves, our families, life in general, and God. Just as Jessie came to the conclusion that God didn't hear her prayers because she didn't feel forgiven, when we start with negative emotions, we end up with negative attitudes and reactions, and wrong thought patterns which cause us to come to wrong conclusions.

For example, *I feel guilty* (negative emotion). That leads to negative reactions such as *I must have something to be guilty about,* and wrong thinking about God: *He can't possibly love me in spite of what the Bible says.* That leads to more wrong conclusions such as: *God is not to be trusted, nor is his Word. I don't believe him.*

Let's reverse that order. Begin with truth: God's Word says God is love, he is a forgiving God, and there is now no condemnation for those who are in Christ Jesus. That is truth, fact, reality. Accepting and believing it leads to positive reactions and attitudes based on truth: *I can accept his love which he freely offers; I am grateful to him*. That results in positive emotions: peace and joy. Start with negative emotions — come to wrong conclusions about truth. Start with truth — come to right conclusions and have positive emotions.

A perfect example of negative emotions producing wrong conclusions is found in the story of Mary and Martha in Luke 10:38-42. We've all heard the story of these two sisters who, along with their brother Lazarus, were beloved friends of Jesus. But there is also an element to this familiar story that speaks to the idea of emotions overriding reason and causing wrong thinking about God.

Martha is described in various translations as being anxious, distracted, troubled, worried and upset — all negative emotions — about the serving. Reasoning from her emotions, Martha came to a wrong conclusion about Jesus — that he didn't care about her or her situation. 'Lord, *don't you care* that my sister has left me to do the work by myself?' she asks him. We don't know for sure how long Jesus had known the family, but Martha knew him well enough to call him 'Lord'. The Greek word translated 'Lord' means literally 'supreme in authority', so clearly she was aware of his power and position, if not his deity. Surely by this time, in the latter part of his ministry, Martha would have known of his teachings, as well as his miracles. Surely she knew that this was no ordinary man, but someone of incredible power who healed all manner of disease, who forgave sin, and who had compassion on the poor and weak and afflicted. These were all things she *knew*. And yet she *felt* that he didn't care about her. Although she and her brother and sister were part of his small circle of close friends who knew him intimately, what Martha knew intellectually about Jesus was erased by her strong emotions. Her starting point was her negative emotions and the result was an incorrect conclusion about Jesus, that he didn't care about her.

So often, women are overwhelmed by emotions that overpower their ability to think and reason clearly. I once taught a math class for women who had dropped out of high school and were attempting to rebuild their basic skills in order to enter the work force. These women had failed most of their math exams and those repeated failures had produced in them severe cases of 'math anxiety'. Their emotional responses to math actually made learning the subject impossible because the cognitive processes required to perform math tasks are inhibited by emotional responses to mathematical functions. Their overpowering negative emotions about math inhibited their ability to use the reasoning parts of their brains to solve math problems. Emotion is a chemical reaction in the brain which we experience as basic 'feelings'. Those same chemicals inhibit our higher cognitive capabilities and limit rational thought. Simply put, we cannot think and feel at the same time. This is why Martha's accusation of Jesus was not based on reason. Her emotions dictated her thoughts instead of the other way around. In short, she allowed her emotions to control her reason, instead of the other way around.

As I said before, we don't want to try to rid ourselves of our emotions, but neither can we allow them to control us. Fear and doubt must not win out over what we know to be true by faith. Ideally, when we have strong negative feelings, there should be a little voice in the back of our minds saying, 'These feelings are very powerful, but they are lying to me.' Again, the goal is not to eliminate emotions but to be able to recognize them for what they are — compelling and persuasive, but no match for God's truth.

5

Nothing to fear but fear itself:

Fear

While speaking at a women's retreat, I asked those in attendance to write down one or two things that they fear most. As expected, the common fears of women came up often: fear of serious illness and death, both of ourselves and our loved ones; fears about children — having them, not having them, what will happen to them and become of them; fear of doing the wrong thing/making wrong decisions; fear of natural disasters out of our control.

As Christians, the question we struggle with is: Who or what determines whether these things happen? Who or what causes anything to happen in our lives? If we don't know, then we face the future fearfully because fear of the unknown is the greatest stress producer in life. That's why it's important to have a clear understanding of who or what controls the events of our lives, and there are only a limited number of possibilities — God, people (including us), demonic forces, and random chance. Having a settled conviction about who's driving the train of our existence is the key to conquering fear.

Let's dispense with random chance at the outset. Chance can't be the cause of anything because chance is not a force. When we flip a coin, we say there is a 50/50 chance that it will come up heads. But chance doesn't cause the coin to come up heads. Whoever flips it sets it in motion and the force with which it's flipped determines how many times it turns over in the air. That, combined with the weight of the coin and the distance it travels in the air, determines which side it lands on. Chance causes nothing because chance has no determining will to do anything and no power to make it come to pass.

So we've eliminated chance as the controller of our lives and destiny, and, along with it, the fear that comes from thinking no one is in charge and we are in the hands of fate or random chance. So we are left with God, us, others, and Satan as the possible controllers of the events of our lives.

So often we want to think that we are in control and that we have the freedom to do as we please, to plan our own futures and to orchestrate the symphony of our own lives. But when the storms of life hit, when a loved one dies, when terminal illness strikes, when an accident finds us rushing to the hospital, when jobs are lost and the bills begin to pile up, when friends reject and hurt us, where is our freedom then? Do we really want to turn to our 'freedom' for comfort?

How free are we?

I received a dreaded phone call from my husband's employer one morning telling me he had been injured in a construction accident and I was needed at the hospital. I was working for one of the largest Christian ministries in the country at the time, and I turned to my co-workers, briefly explained the situation, and asked them to pray. As I was driving to the hospital, I felt an overwhelming sense of absolute helplessness. All I knew from the phone call was that neck and back injuries were involved, and the prospect of my husband being paralyzed and possibly dying loomed large in my mind. I had no freedom to influence events. I was utterly helpless. I could barely choke out a few feeble prayers, although I didn't even know what to pray. But the Spirit interceded for me 'with groans that words cannot express' (Rom. 8:26), and God's sovereign control of all events in life sustained us through the next few hours and the next months as Tom recovered from a broken back.

We're not free from sickness, pain, heartache and death. So are we really free at all? Do we really control our lives and our destinies? More importantly, do we really want to? I give you this scenario: you have two choices. You can either give control of your life over to a sinful, unpredictable, unreliable person whose wisdom is limited, who frequently makes bad choices, and whose decisions are often swayed by emotion, OR you give control of your life over to an all-wise, all-knowing, all-powerful, gracious, merciful, loving person who has nothing but good intentions for you. Which would you choose? You'd have to be crazy to choose the first. But when we insist on trying to control our own lives, that is exactly what we do.

Do we really want to turn to our free will as our comfort in hard times? We like the idea of free will when it's our free will, but when others' free wills stomp on our free will, it's not so appealing. But that's what you get when you see free will as sovereign. If your will is free, then so is mine and that of your rotten boss, the crook with a gun, terrorists, and every other evil creature in the world. And that means our lives are in their hands, not our own. Does that kind of thinking make us strong and fearless?

Satan's control

Now we've also eliminated chance and human free will as controllers of our lives. Some people find it appealing to think that Satan has control over a certain amount of life, and that God is constantly revising his plans to accommodate Satan's tricks. Is that a comforting thought? Does the idea that Satan has control over any part of your life make you fearless? Remember the book of Job. Satan came to God and said, 'Job only serves you because you protect him.' So God gave him permission to do certain things to Job, to test him up to a certain point, but no farther. Could Satan do more than that? No.

God is in control over Satan and his demons who try to thwart his plans at every step. It's easy for us to see that because we have the book of Job and we know all that was taking place, both in heaven and on earth. But Job and his friends were in the dark. After they questioned God about the apparent injustice of Job's plight for thirty-seven chapters, God finally spoke. But did he say, 'Ok, Job. Now I'm going to explain it all to you'? No. He said, 'Where were you when I created the world?' Job saw that he really hadn't understood God, that he has a plan and a purpose, and that all we need to know about it is that it's perfect because he is perfect.

Satan knew from the Old Testament that God's plan was for Jesus to come to the earth, be betrayed, crucified and resurrected, and provide salvation for millions, and if there was any way to keep that from happening, Satan would have done it. If just one of the hundreds of prophecies about the Messiah could have been caused by Satan to fail to come to pass, the whole plan would have collapsed. But the numbers of independent decisions made by thousands of people were used by God to bring his plan to pass in exactly the way he had designed it from the beginning, and Satan couldn't do a thing about it.

No action by the Romans, the Pharisees, Judas, or anyone else kept God's plan from unfolding exactly the way he purposed it from before the foundation of the world. Ephesians 1 says we were chosen in him for salvation before the world was even created and before sin even entered the minds of Adam and Eve. That means God knit together Satan's rebellion, Adam and Eve's sin, the fall of the human race, and the death and crucifixion of Christ — all seemingly terrible events — to shower his love on us and save us before he even created us! Here is a perfect example of God working all things together for good (Rom. 8:28). Unlimited in power, unrivalled in majesty, and not limited by anything outside himself, our God is in complete control of all circumstances, causing or allowing them for his own good purposes and plans to be fulfilled exactly as he has foreordained.

How does the way we look at who is in control of our lives affect our relationship with God? As Christians, the things we fear most can cause our faith to collide directly with the God we say we believe in. If they happen, the first thing we ask is *Why?* or *Why me, Lord?* or *How could you let this happen?* Then we may begin to wonder about God himself. Is he there? Does he care about me? Does he know what's happening to me? Is he in control? Is he good?

Each of these questions can be answered in absolute certainty if we know our God, if we know his attributes and his nature well enough to have a settled inner certainty that we can trust him and trust what he says. I've known my husband for over thirty-five years and I know what he will and won't do. I trust him implicitly because I've seen him in action and because he has proven himself to be trustworthy all these years. I've experienced his love, his faithfulness, his goodness, and I never fear that he will do something evil or unkind or something that is not in my best interest. That's what we need to be able to say about God.

When the worst happens

Terrible events in our lives will either confirm what we know about God — that he is good, he does care about us and, most of all, that he is in control — or they will devastate us, our faith, and our witness to the world. And while we know we cannot lose our salvation, we can lose our joy and be set adrift on a sea of ever-increasing fears and terrors. Which will you be? And how can you make sure you are in the first group? How can we be formidable, fearless women of faith? Is it even possible?

64

*Know God.
Know His Word.*

Hosea 4:6 says, 'My people are destroyed from lack of knowledge. Because you have rejected knowledge, I also reject you as my priests.' This was spoken by God to the Israelites and their leaders who kept the knowledge of the true God from the people and led them to worship idols. But we don't even have that excuse. The knowledge of God, the same intimate knowledge of him that we have of our loved ones, is available to us. We have the Bible, his revelation to us about himself. We have leaders who teach us the knowledge of the true God. To not take advantage of it, to fail to know God through his Word, to ignore the teaching of our leaders, is to destroy ourselves.

This doesn't mean we lose our salvation for lack of knowledge. Rather, the Greek word translated 'destroyed' also means 'to fail, be undone, cast down, made silent'. God's people fail and are cast down and undone by the trials of life, our fears are magnified, and our witness is silenced for lack of the intimate, personal knowledge of our God, not for lack of emotional experiences, or the lack of more potlucks, bigger churches, more musical performances, more and bigger stuff in our lives, or more activities. We are destroyed by a lack of knowledge of our Creator, because real, intimate knowledge of God is the life of the soul, true life, eternal life, as Jesus said in his prayer for his disciples, 'Now this is eternal life: that they may know you, the only true God, and Jesus Christ, whom you have sent' (John 17:3).

I am absolutely convinced that nothing gives a woman strength and confidence and alleviates her fears like an understanding of the sovereignty of God in her life. God's sovereignty is defined as his complete and total independent control over every creature, event and circumstance at every moment in history. Subject to none, influenced by none, absolutely independent, God does what he pleases, only as he pleases, and always as he pleases. Best of all, what he pleases to do is always perfect and holy.

If you are bristling at this, understand that this is, and always has been, a very unpopular subject in Christian circles. But it is particularly unpopular in the West where freedom is the highest virtue. But isn't it better to know and believe what the Bible says, that God is in complete control of every molecule in the universe at every moment, and everything that happens is either caused by him or allowed by him for his own perfect purposes? Let's look at some passages that explain this.

First, God has sovereign control over the plans he has made and nothing and no one can thwart those plans:

- *Isaiah 14:24*: 'The LORD almighty has sworn, "Surely, as I have planned, so it will be, and as I have purposed, so it will stand."' Nothing is random or comes by chance, especially not in the lives of believers. He 'purposed' it. To 'purpose' means to deliberately resolve to do something. God has resolved to do what he will do and nothing and no one stands in his way.

- *Isaiah 46:10*: 'I make known the end from the beginning, from ancient times, what is still to come. I say: "My purpose will stand, and I will do all that I please."' This is our powerful, purposeful God who is in control of everything. That should bring us great comfort and help to alleviate our fears.

If we don't feel comfortable with him having all that control, it's because we don't know him, we aren't sure of the rest of his attributes. A completely sovereign God who is also merciless, angry and unpredictable would be a nightmare. But our God is not only sovereign, he is also good, compassionate, loving and immutable. He does not change like shifting shadows but remains eternally faithful, our Rock and our Redeemer.

God's total sovereignty over all creation directly contradicts the philosophy of open theism, which states that God doesn't know what's going to happen in the future any more than we do, so he has to be constantly changing his plans and reacting to what the sinful creatures do as they exercise their free will. But God isn't finding out what's going to happen as events unfold. He is continuously, actively running things — ALL things — here and now. But to think he needs our cooperation, our help, or the exercise of our free will to bring his plans to pass puts us in control over him, which makes us God. Where have we heard that lie before? It's Satan's old lie from the Garden again: 'you shall be like God' (Gen. 3:5). Any time you hear a philosophy that gives you power over God in any form, that allows you to act outside of his will and plan, remember Genesis 3:5.

But does God even have control over presidents and prime ministers and dictators, those who rule the world through governments? King Nebuchadnezzar found this out, as described in Daniel 4:28-37. Verses 34-35 contain the truth that Nebuchadnezzar needed to learn — that God's dominion (kingdom) is eternal, he does what he pleases with the 'powers of heaven and peoples of the earth' and no one can stop him. 'The Most High is sovereign over the kingdoms of men and gives them to anyone he wishes and sets over them the lowliest of men' (Dan. 4:17). No earthly ruler can override God's plans and purpose. Our response should be as Nebuchadnezzar's — to praise and honor and glorify him (v. 37), not just because he's in sovereign control, but because he is also right and just and holy and perfect and good. Can you imagine that kind of power in the hands of an evil, unjust god? Or a god that really doesn't care about us? But we can rejoice and take comfort in our God's sovereignty because it is overshadowed by his goodness, his love, his mercy and his holiness.

God's sovereignty and our fears

So what does God's sovereignty mean to us and our lives and how does it make us fearless? Hebrews 12:1 says, '…let us throw off everything that hinders and the sin that so easily entangles, and let us run with perseverance the race marked out for us.' Some versions say 'the race set before us'. It means appointed, made up in advance. Think of it as a ski racer barreling down a slalom course weaving in and out of the gates on the course that has been set in advance. Jeremiah 29:11 adds: '"For I know the plans I have for you," declares the LORD, "plans to prosper you and not to harm you, plans to give you hope and a future."' We don't wander through life directionless. We live according to God's plan for us. Even when we sin and think we are out of God's will, he still controls our rebellion and, if we are truly his children, he guides us back onto the path of his perfect plan.

A lot of women live with the unconscious sense that if God has a plan for them, something needs to happen before they can get on with the plan. That's the Plan A/Plan B paradigm. Single women think: '*I can't really begin to live God's plan (Plan A) for me until the right guy comes along. So for now I'm stuck in Plan B.*' There is this sense among single women that they are living a second-class life of no use to God until they are married. After speaking on this very topic at a women's retreat, I received a note from one of the attendees: '*Thank you for reminding me that being single at age thirty-two is God's best Plan A for me. And I hope you keep reminding me to RELAX and let God be God in bringing me a husband.*' By the time the next retreat rolled around a year later, she was married to a godly man who was preparing for the ministry.

A married woman may think God's Plan A for her can only be fulfilled when she has children. Or she may feel that she is just playing a supporting role in the drama her husband is starring in, but God doesn't really have a plan for her. Or a married woman may invest her life in her children and watch them grow up to fulfil God's plan for them, but she feels there really isn't a plan of her own beyond that. Or the divorced or widowed woman believes God's plan for her is on hold unless she remarries. The young girl thinks she can't start living God's best plan for her until she graduates from high school or college. But if God has marked out the race for us, then every day of our lives has meaning and purpose because God has planned it that way. No matter how intertwined our lives are in the lives of husbands, children, or the husbands and children or careers yet to come, we are still on a personal, individual journey with God. There is no Plan B for the Christian woman; we are all living in Plan A right now.

We do not have to wait for circumstances to change in order to live in Plan A. God's control of all circumstances makes that clear. If something hasn't happened yet, it's because God's timing hasn't brought it to pass yet. And since he is perfect, his timing is perfect. So to the single woman, I say *relax*. Live in the plan God has for you now and trust that his plan will unfold in exactly the way he has ordained it. To the married woman, don't wait for your husband's plan to be fulfilled before you seek to fulfill God's plan for you. Don't wait for your children to grow and leave home before you live God's plan for you. Yes, be a supportive, nurturing mom and wife, but seek God's plan for you to become his intimate ally. Knowing these truths about God's sovereignty gives us great comfort and makes our fears seem so much less troubling. So where is fear and worrying? Are you worried about your possessions? Psalm 50:10: 'For every animal of the forest is mine, and the cattle on a thousand hills.' Your possessions are not yours anyway. They're his. Let him worry about them. Let your requests be known to God with prayer and supplication; then trust him to provide what you need. That's the way to the peace that passes all understanding (Phil. 4:6-7). Job 41:11 says, 'Who has a claim against me that I must pay? Everything under heaven belongs to me.' God owes us nothing. He owns everything, even the children he lends to us for a short time in order to mature them and us into the people he has planned us all to be.

Worried about the politicians and how they can't seem to govern with wisdom and concern for the people? Remember Psalm 75:6-7 (NKJV): 'For exaltation [Heb. "promotion"] comes neither from the east nor from the west nor from the south. But God is the Judge: he puts down one, and exalts another.' Daniel 2:21 (NKJV) says, 'And he changes the times and the seasons; he removes kings and raises up kings; he gives wisdom to the wise and knowledge to those who have understanding.' But they're ruining the country! Maybe they are, but they're not doing it outside the plan of God. Maybe the country will be bankrupt and powerless and maybe that's the reason the West isn't mentioned in prophecy as part of the battle of Armageddon. Whatever happens, it's not going to come as a shock to God.

The Lord Jesus certainly found solace in God's sovereignty. He wasn't answering Pontius Pilate's questions. 'Do you refuse to speak to me?' Pilate said. 'Don't you realize I have power either to free you or to crucify you?' Jesus answered: 'You would have no power over me if it were not given to you from above' (John 19:10-11). Jesus knew where the power was and who was in charge of the plan.

So if you want to be a woman who is formidable, strong and fearless, know your God. Know his attributes, know what he has done in the past, and be confident in him. Daniel 11:32b says, 'The people who know their God will firmly resist him.' I like the ESV translation: 'but the people who know their God shall stand firm and take action.' There's only one way to know God — through his Word. There is no magic formula to make you a spiritual giant by using seven steps to spiritual growth, no mystical prayer that you can pray three times a day to mature you, build your faith and make you a formidable tower of strength. I don't have a quick formula to make you a fearless woman in the world. All I have is the source of power that will change your life from the inside out. But it takes effort — diligent, everyday effort — to know the God who controls everything. Drink deeply of his Word and let it fill your minds and hearts. A woman whose heart is filled with God and his Word will find there is no room in her heart for fear.

6

Can you believe it?!:

Doubt

I once received a frantic e-mail from a woman named Dianne who had struggled for years with doubts:

> *How do you get rid of the doubts????? I`ve been struggling for SO LONG now, I`ve begun to wonder if my chance has already passed! How do I know God is there at all? Sometimes I wonder!! How do I know he loves me? How can others just accept that He is in their lives when I don't see Him at all? And God is all powerful and can do anything, right? So why couldn't he just forgive us of our sins and not have Jesus die? I understand that He is a just God and that a price has to be paid, but why can't he just not do that since He can do anything? It doesn't make sense. I give up!!!!*

This poor woman has so many doubts about God, his nature and his plans that she doesn't know where to turn. Doubt can be a very powerful emotion, as it is in her life, as we see from the number of exclamation points she uses!!! But as chapter 4 makes clear, overwhelming emotion always makes rational, objective thinking about God difficult. We women are so much at the mercy of our emotions that we often cannot think clearly. When doubts take over our minds and emotions, our hearts become tangled and produce even greater emotions, more doubts, wrong thinking, and faulty conclusions.

Everyone doubts at one time or another and not all doubt is negative. There are some types of doubt which are constructive and are in fact encouraged in the Bible. Some level of skepticism is healthy and justified. When we hear claims of health, wealth and prosperity, for instance, we should receive the information suspiciously because much of it contradicts what has been clearly revealed in Scripture — that the Christian life is a battle, that man is born to trouble as the sparks fly upward (Job 5:7) and that following Christ *will* involve persecution (2 Tim. 3:12). Furthermore, God never promises his children health, wealth or prosperity, at least not in the temporal sense. Like Paul, we suffer from various thorns in the flesh. Like Jesus, who had no place to rest his head, many Christians live in circumstances of severe poverty. But God did promise peace with him, joy in the journey, love abounding to us and in us, and healthy spirits and true wealth — the precious gift of eternal life. But when we fall for the lie that is the prosperity gospel and we don't get all the promised 'goodies', then the doubts about God come creeping in.

As in the case of faulty claims, doubt can be a valuable element in honest evaluation. Healthy doubt prevents us from coming to hasty conclusions or making commitments to unreliable and untrustworthy sources. Doubting outrageous statements, waiting for sufficient evidence before accepting something, analyzing claims and comparing them to truth — all are constructive and beneficial types of doubt. This type of wholesome skepticism characterized the Bereans who examined the Scriptures to see if what Paul was saying was true (Acts 17:11). In fact, because of their skepticism and the joy with which they received what was really true, they were considered by Paul to be of 'noble character'.

The Bible also exhorts us to be doubtful about our own abilities, especially our ability to do, in our own power, anything of value in the kingdom of God. Nowhere in Scripture are we *ever* told to have faith in ourselves or our capacity to accomplish anything of worth. In fact, just the opposite is true. If we understand that our hearts are 'deceitful ... and desperately wicked' (Jer. 17:9, NKJV), then we will agree with Paul and have 'no confidence in the flesh' (Phil. 3:3). So doubting ourselves and our human skills and facilities, especially as they apply to the spiritual life, is wise. It's when that doubt spills over into misgivings and reservations about God that it becomes devastating and destructive.

Dianne's e-mail indicates just such a doubt. When she asks: '*Why couldn't he just forgive us of our sins and not have Jesus die?*', her doubts cross over into the realm of sin. She admits that God is all powerful and can do anything, yet she questions his right to do exactly as he pleases. Can she, or any mere mortal, possibly have a better plan than the perfect plan which came from the mind of the Almighty? It is true that we cannot expect to understand that mind perfectly, as he reminds us in Isaiah 55:8-9: '"For my thoughts are not your thoughts, neither are your ways my ways," declares the LORD. "As the heavens are higher than the earth, so are my ways higher than your ways and my thoughts than your thoughts." But when we doubt any aspect of God's nature,

Doubt =
Unbelief =
Sin

especially his trustworthiness, or we doubt what he has revealed to us in his Word, or we question his perfect will and purposes, then doubt can only be defined as sin. It is the opposite of faith and 'everything that does not come from faith is sin' (Rom. 14:23). Like any sin, however, it can be quickly confessed and forgiven.

Doubting our own salvation

One of the most common doubts that surfaces in the spiritual life is the doubt about our own salvation. In one sense, this is a positive thing. Some people who doubt their salvation do so because they're not really saved. A dear friend relates that she spent twenty years in a 'mainline' church where the social life was full and busy. Everyone assumed she was a Christian, but no one ever asked her if that was true. There was no urging to examine herself to see if she was truly in the faith and, as it turned out, she wasn't. When she finally heard an explanation of the true gospel, beginning with sin and separation from God and ending with the sacrifice of Christ on the cross for that sin, she repented and gave her life to Jesus. As Paul urged, we are to examine ourselves to see if we truly are 'in the faith' (2 Cor. 13:5). And if doubts about our salvation have a legitimate cause, the only course of action is to come to Christ in repentance and faith. Those who do will never be rejected by him: 'Whoever comes to me I will never drive away' (John 6:37). But once we have experienced the cleansing from sin that only Jesus provides, we are not to continue living in doubt.

Why do Christians doubt their salvation? There are several possibilities, and if you doubt your salvation or you are counseling someone who does, it's helpful to know why. Primarily, a saved person who still doubts her salvation usually doesn't have a true understanding of the gospel. She may believe faith is a work she has to accomplish, rather than a gift from God (Eph. 2:8-9). Some believe that salvation is a gift, but after they are saved, they believe maintaining their salvation is a matter of their effort. Any failure to live a perfect, sinless life causes them to question the validity of their salvation. They misapply the words, 'I can do all things through Christ who strengthens me' with a heavy emphasis on *I can do*. When they fail to *do*, they doubt themselves and their salvation. They just do not understand the magnitude of being 'in Christ'.

Second, if a person doubts their salvation, it could be that they have been raised in a home or church where confrontational, convicting preaching or teaching has not been balanced by strong teaching about the grace of God to undeserving sinners. For sensitive souls with a strong natural sense of guilt, this can produce a relentless sense of sin so enormous that they feel they can't possibly live up to the standard. Frankly, this doesn't happen all that often today. Generally speaking, the day of the pulpit-pounding, 'hell fire and brimstone' preacher is a thing of the past.

Third, some people feel they are too sinful to be saved. They don't understand the scope of the cross or the depth of the love of God toward sinners. Too many people listen to the whispering of demons in their ears telling them God can't possibly save them because their sins are too great. This is one of Satan's favorite lies. He gets us thinking we have to 'do' something to clean up our act before God will save us, and then convinces us nothing we can do is good enough. That way we stay on his evil little merry-go-round, chasing our tails into an eternity in hell. This is also sometimes a result of reverse pride that says, 'I'm special — SO sinful that even the Creator of the universe can't save me.' This comes from an exalted view of self and a limited view of God. No sin is so great that it cannot be covered by the blood of Christ. The love of God, according to the old hymn, is 'greater far than tongue or pen can ever tell. It goes beyond the highest star and reaches to the lowest hell.' No one is too sinful to be saved.

Some doubt their salvation because they have convinced themselves that every little thing has to be confessed in order to be forgiven. They obsess about every thought, word and action, trying to determine if it is sin and needs to be confessed. They don't understand the completeness of the forgiveness in Christ, that he paid the penalty for all sins — past, present, future. They don't understand that we have died with Christ and are resurrected with him to 'walk in the newness of life'. That means we're completely new creatures. Sin has no hold on us. Yes, we still sin, but we don't have to obsess about it and fall on our knees every time a stray sinful thought crosses our minds.

Both Martin Luther and John Bunyan, the author of *The Pilgrim's Progress*, suffered from a disproportionate sense of guilt over unwanted thoughts that crept into their minds continually. Once they clearly understood the truth that 'there is now no condemnation for those who are in Christ Jesus' (Rom. 8:1), both were released from their torment and went on to become giants of the faith whose influence is still felt today.

Closely related to this is the keen awareness of the flesh that causes some to believe they cannot possibly be saved and still have sinful thoughts and desires. They don't understand the nature of the continual battle of the flesh against the spirit. The apostle Paul suffered the same ravages of the battle against the flesh, as he attests in Romans 7: 'I do not understand what I do. For what I want to do I do not do, but what I hate I do' (v. 15). But rather than doubt that his salvation was real, he cried out to God, 'Who will rescue me from this body of death?' and then answered his own question. It is only 'through Jesus Christ our Lord!' that we can have victory in the battle against the sin nature (vv. 24-25).

Believers often doubt their salvation because of the trials they experience, which they see as evidence God is not present in their lives. They lack the understanding of the role of trials in the Christian life, seeing them as either punishment from a God who is not pleased with them or evidence God isn't in their lives at all. *If he were*, they reason, *this wouldn't be happening to me*. That simply isn't true. The Christian life is a spiritual battle and trials are put into our lives by God to mature our faith and increase our dependence upon him. The trials 'have come so that your faith — of greater worth than gold, which perishes even though refined by fire — may be proved genuine and may result in praise, glory and honor when Jesus Christ is revealed' (1 Peter 1:7).

Why believers doubt God

Many Christian women, even though they have a settled assurance of their own salvation, still live with continual doubts about God. Their doubts rise up in the night to rob them of sleep as they ponder the question of God's nature and plans for them. *Doesn't God know how I'm suffering/worrying/fearing? How can*

Can you believe it?

God love me if I'm going through this? Why doesn't he answer my
prayers? Is he strong enough to carry me through? Does he want
to? Does he even care about me?

These questions arise in the hearts of God's children, even after
times of amazing spiritual victories and 'highs', just as they did
in the hearts of Peter and the disciples. In one unforgettable
incident, Peter and the disciples were on the lake in their boat
waiting for Jesus who had gone into the hills to pray. After
feeding 5000 men (and no doubt thousands of women and
children as well) in a miraculous display of creative power, Jesus
needed some solitude in which to commune with his Father.
When evening came, the wind howled and the boat was tossed
and 'buffeted by the waves'. As experienced fishermen, the
disciples were well aware of the danger posed to a small boat
by fierce winds.

But as it was nearing the dawn, they saw Jesus walking across
the water toward them. Their reaction was quite naturally one
of terror that he might be a ghost (Matt. 14:25-26). But Peter,
ever the impulsive one but filled with love for his Lord, asked
permission to get out of the boat and walk on the water to
Jesus. We can imagine the joy he experienced as he found
himself doing the impossible. But suddenly the wind and waves
caused him to look at his circumstances through the eyes of
doubt and disbelief. 'But when he saw the wind, he was afraid
and, beginning to sink, cried out, "Lord, save me!" Immediately
Jesus reached out his hand and caught him. "You of little faith,"
he said, "why did you doubt?"'

Why exactly did Peter doubt? Mark's account of the feeding of
the 5000, although it doesn't mention Peter by name, gives us

the clue. The disciples 'were completely amazed, for they had not understood about the loaves; their hearts were hardened' (Mark 6:51-52). The doubts of Peter and the disciples had the same basis as the doubts of all believers — an incomplete, immature faith born out of a shallow, undeveloped understanding of God. The disciples had just witnessed an extraordinary miracle, and yet they did not fully understand what they had seen, nor did they truly know and understand the One whose power had brought the miracle to pass. Their hearts were 'hardened', but not in the sense that Pharaoh's heart was hardened against God, or the Pharisees' hearts were hardened because of their pride and self-righteousness. Rather, this hardening of the heart is due to a faith that is small, untested and weak. Even after Christ was crucified and resurrected, he appeared to the Eleven (Judas having died by this time) and they worshiped him, but *some still doubted*! (Matt. 28:16-17).

These were believers, followers of Christ, chosen by him and saved by his work on the cross. But still they doubted. They had faith, but it was 'little faith', not the faith that moves mountains. In their first encounter with wind and waves when Jesus was asleep in their boat, they woke him up crying, 'Lord, save us! We're going to drown!' Jesus rebuked the winds and asked: 'You of little faith, why are you so afraid?' (Matt. 8:25-26). Their small faith in the identity of the Man they followed, their incomplete understanding that here was God in flesh dwelling among them, was evident in their reaction: 'The men were amazed and asked: "What kind of man is this? Even the winds and the waves obey him!"' (v. 27). Here then is the reason that we doubt, even though we know Christ, belong to him and follow him. Our faith is simply too small. We don't truly know him in all his glory and power. It's not that we don't have faith;

it's that the faith we have is not sufficient for the tasks and trials that lie in our paths.

When I first married my husband, I carried over many doubts from a previous relationship with a man who had proved to be untrustworthy and unfaithful. Naturally I expected the man I married to be entirely different, but I still waited to see if that would be true. The jury was still out. Now, after thirty-five years of marriage, my doubts have been completely erased because I have seen Tom in action. I have experienced his faithfulness, his honesty, his complete trustworthiness. In short, because I *know him*, I never doubt him. We simply must be able to say the same about God. The disciples who doubted didn't know him well enough. But that was about to change.

Peter's transformation

Peter's doubts surfaced again and again in his life, culminating in his ultimate experience of doubt and fear the night of Jesus' arrest. Hiding in fear and denying even knowing Jesus three times, he eventually was overcome by remorse and 'went outside and wept bitterly' (Matt. 26:75). But after the resurrection and the coming of the Holy Spirit upon believers at Pentecost, we see a different Peter. The book of Acts shows us a 'new and improved' Peter, one who boldly proclaims the truth about Christ before the Sanhedrin and refuses to be silenced (Acts 2 and 4), who heals with miraculous power (Acts 3:1-10), and who became one of the pillars of the Jerusalem church. He went on to write the books of 1 and 2 Peter and remained a formidable force of faith throughout the rest of his life. Although the Bible doesn't tell us how Peter died, the accepted church tradition is that he was crucified upside-down on a cross in Rome in fulfillment of Jesus' prophecy (John 21:18). When Peter was put to death, we are told that he requested that he might be crucified with his head downward, saying that he who had denied his Lord as he had done was not worthy to die as he did.

What happened to Peter between those times of doubting and the rest of his life? What made the difference? What did he do that we can do to end our doubts? One thing is for certain. Peter didn't follow the advice of too many retreat and conference speakers, especially the high-powered, type-A personalities who own successful ministries and pump out books by the dozen. He didn't simply 'make a commitment' to being fearless. He didn't just 'decide' to be a strong, faithful follower of Christ. He didn't 'make up his mind' to stop doubting or tell himself, 'You can do it, Peter!' Those things may work for the high-powered crowd, but not for Peter, and not for the average woman. And he certainly never tried 'speaking words of faith', as some advocate, which is nothing more than the secular 'power of positive confession' couched in Christian terms.

Peter himself explains the transformation in his response to the crowd who saw him heal the crippled beggar in the temple court in Acts 3: 'Why does this surprise you? Why do you stare at us *as if by our own power or godliness* we had made this man walk?' (v. 12, emphasis added). You see, Peter knew that it was not in his power to overcome his doubts, no more than it was his power that healed the crippled man. Along with thousands at Pentecost, Peter had been given the gift of the Holy Spirit, who came to live in the hearts of all believers in Christ, the same Spirit that lives in us today! This is what changed Peter from a doubting, fearful man into a pillar of strength. The same Father

82

Can you believe it?

God who gives us the gift of salvation (Eph. 2:8-9) gives us the gift of the Holy Spirit at the moment of salvation. His Spirit lives in our hearts, bringing us power to 'do all things through Christ who strengthens' and reminding us of the things we have learned about God (John 14:26). No doubt Peter's mind was flooded with the memories of his time with Jesus — his power to heal and save, his love and care for his own, his promise to remain with us 'always, to the very end of the age' (Matt. 28:20).

The Spirit functions the same way for each of us, only today we don't think back on firsthand experiences of walking with Jesus along the dusty roads of Palestine. Rather, he directs us to something even better — the complete Word of God. Peter acknowledges this in 2 Peter 1:16-21 where he describes his miraculous experience on the Mount of the Transfiguration (Matt. 17:1-8). Not even seeing Jesus in his glorified state talking with Moses and Elijah compares to the 'word of the prophets made more certain'. The Word of God, the Bible, is all we need to make us 'complete, thoroughly equipped for every good work' (2 Tim. 3:17, NKJV). The woman who is complete and thoroughly equipped is not plagued by doubts and fears. She is freed from them, as Jesus promised in John 8:31-32: 'If you hold to my teaching, you are really my disciples. Then you will know the truth, and the truth will set you free.' Our job is to so saturate our minds and hearts with the truths of God's Word that they free us from the bondage of doubts.

Only by the miraculous power of the truths of Scripture can we stand on the solid rock of the foundation of our faith; not our own faith, but the faith that is the gift of God, a faith which will grow and mature as we spend more and more time in the Word. We primarily know God through what he has revealed in

83

the Bible about himself, his nature, his character, his mind and his heart. But if we neglect him by neglecting his revelation of himself, we will find doubts, fears and anxieties crowding out the settled assurance about him and his love and plans for us.

⟶ Two types of doubters

Perhaps you have heard a sermon or read about James's assessment of the one who doubts, that he is 'like a wave of the sea, blown and tossed by the wind. That man should not think he will receive anything from the Lord; he is a double-minded man, unstable in all he does' (James 1:6-8). Perhaps you have feared that because of your doubts, you will miss out on God's blessings and displease him. The Greek word for 'doubt' in the James passage is not the same one Jesus used about Peter and the disciples. Jesus asked Peter why he 'doubted', using the Greek word *distazo*, which means 'double standing' and implies uncertainty as to which way to go. It is said of believers whose faith is small. Jesus was asking, in effect, 'Peter, why are you behaving like an unbeliever? Stop dithering around and follow me in the way. Grow up and be strong in your faith.' *Distazo* is used again in Matthew 28:17 of the disciples who worshiped him, even though some doubted. This is not the doubt of unbelievers, but of believers with weak and immature faith.

But James doesn't use *distazo* to describe the double-minded man who will not receive anything from the Lord. The verb the Holy Spirit causes him to choose is *diakrino*, which means literally 'to withdraw from or, by implication, to oppose'. This is the person who has withdrawn from believing and following Christ, the person who is blown off course by his doubts, never to return. He is represented by the second and third soils in the parable of the sower (Matt. 13), the one who 'receives the Word with joy' but because of the cares of the world or the deceitfulness of riches, he falls away. This Greek word suggests not so much weakness of faith as the lack of it.

Abraham, who was a true believer, did not 'waver' (*diakrino*) because of doubt. The promises of God that he and Sarah would have a child in their old age were unbelievable, 'Yet he did not waver through unbelief regarding the promise of God, but was strengthened in his faith and gave glory to God, being fully persuaded that God had power to do what he had promised' (Rom. 4:20-21). Did Abraham's faith rest in his own power to accomplish the impossible? No. His confidence was in the same power that Peter saw at work in the healing of the crippled beggar — the power of Almighty God, the Creator of the universe in whom all power rests. That very same power is available to us to dispel our doubts and make us strong and assured women of God. His power is the only power able to do that.

Dispelling our doubts

Whether from outright unbelief in the non-Christian or from weak faith in the believer, doubt is sin because it does not come from faith (Rom. 14:23). The first step in overcoming doubt is to admit to ourselves that it *is* sin and that it stems from unbelief and confess it to God. When we ask him to forgive our sin, he is 'faithful and just and will forgive us our sins and purify us from all unrighteousness' (1 John 1:9). Many women struggle with the concept of doubt as sin. We prefer to label it a failing, a shortcoming or a limitation. We may also sigh, 'That's just the way I am. I can't help it.' No, we cannot help it. But God can, and he will if we bring it to him in sincerity, admitting that doubt is sin and recognizing that it is possible to overcome doubt through the power of the Spirit.

The next step is to pray for the wisdom (James 1:5), the power and the hope to overcome doubt: 'May the God of hope fill you with all joy and peace as you trust in him, so that you may overflow with hope by the power of the Holy Spirit' (Rom. 15:13). Learning to depend on him in prayer may be the very reason God allows a Christian to doubt. Like the man who brought his demon-possessed child to Jesus but was unsure whether Jesus could actually help him, we must go to God and ask him for more and greater faith to overcome our doubts, crying, 'I do believe; help me overcome my unbelief!' (Mark 9:17-27).

Finally, we must do everything we need to do in order to mature in the faith. We must seek God continually in the Bible through diligent study. Only through the Word can we understand the true nature of God and the extent of the faith he gives as a gift to all his people. Remember that the 'sword of the Spirit' is the Word, the only offensive weapon we have to slay the dragons of doubt that seek to consume us.

7

The unbearable burden:

Guilt

My husband comes from a long line of guilt-ridden Norwegians. For years we have laughed about it. Guilt, he claims, is part of the genetic code of Norwegians and makes him do irrational things like refusing to eat the last portion of anything available to the whole family. Many a time I found a tablespoon of ice cream left in the container or a lone cookie in the jar, or a smidgen of cereal lying forlorn in the bottom of the box. 'Who ate the last of the ice cream?!' was apparently frequently heard in his childhood years, and it has rendered him constitutionally unable to eat the last of anything. Of course, he always ate every last scrap of food on his own plate. The guilt about all those people starving in Africa would have been too much for him to bear.

I never really agreed with the idea of national guilt until I read the results of an interesting experiment in a *Reader's Digest* article. First in big cities and small towns around the United States, and then in Europe, Asia, Canada, Australia, New Zealand and Latin

America, the editors of the magazine dropped temptation in the path of unsuspecting people. They 'lost' more than 1100 wallets to see just how many would be returned. Each contained up to $50 in local currency, along with a name and phone number so that the finder would have no trouble returning the contents. They left the wallets on sidewalks and in phone booths, in front of office buildings, discount stores and churches, in parking lots and restaurants, then sat back and waited.

The results were fascinating. Of all the cities and towns all over the world, in only two were 100% of the wallets returned — Oslo, Norway's capital; and Odense in Denmark. I cannot speak for the Danes, but my husband asserts that the Norwegians couldn't possibly keep the wallets or the cash in them. Keeping them would have produced far too much guilt.

Two types of guilt

Like doubt, guilt is a powerful motivator of behavior and, many times, that's a good thing. But there is a vast difference between moral conscience and what psychologists refer to as 'existential guilt', which is free-floating and non-specific. Moral conscience is that part of the human psyche, in normally developed individuals, that tells us what is right and what is wrong. This innate moral sense is the part of us that passes judgement on the morality or immorality of our actions. It is that part of us which helps us to tell the difference between good and evil, and impels us toward the good. It gives comfort and peace when we do right, and plagues us when we tend toward evil actions. God has placed this moral conscience within mankind and when we violate it, we feel remorse.

When the unsaved person violates the moral conscience, the result is legitimate guilt over sin which, hopefully, drives him to Christ. Without a sense of having violated the law of God, we would never realize our need of the Savior. In the Christian, the conscience, quickened by the indwelling Spirit, rightly identifies sin in our lives. This legitimate guilt drives us to seek forgiveness from God so we can enjoy unbroken communion with him and from others in order to re-establish fellowship which may have been broken by our words or actions.

Existential guilt, on the other hand, exaggerates and distorts our everyday experiences of moral conscience and tangles our hearts in a powerful way. This is unreasonable guilt, that which the psychologists call 'free-floating guilt', the nagging feeling that:

- you are responsible for all the evils that befall you and others;
- you are obligated to help or placate others and if they are not helped or placated, it is your fault;
- you must fix other people, fix their problems, or fix their situations;
- you must in some way pay for every mistake you've ever made, every thoughtless word or wrong action.

This existential guilt is unreasonable because it causes us to feel more guilty than we ought to reasonably feel. It is out of proportion to its cause and the impact on our hearts and minds can be devastating. For one thing, this type of guilt can make you become overly responsible or conscientious, constantly striving to make everything 'ok' for you and everyone around you. The problem is that your sense of what is 'ok' keeps moving. The closer you get to it, the farther away it seems. The bar seems to be continually being raised so that it is always kept just a little out of your reach. You may be compelled to overwork, either in your home, your chosen profession, or in your church. You may give of yourself to an unreasonable extent to the detriment of your health, your interpersonal relationships and/ or your relationship to God. You may be willing to do anything in your attempt to make everyone happy. If someone close to you is unhappy, you automatically assume it is something you have done or said — or not done or said — to bring about their unhappiness. Although you are not the cause of their distress, you still want desperately to relieve that distress and because you can't, you feel guilty and inadequate. Their distress may have nothing whatsoever to do with you, and you may even recognize that, but it makes no difference. Somehow you still feel responsible.

The guilt-ridden person can be overly sensitive to the reactions of others. 'You can't please all the people all the time' is not a phrase you can identify with. You feel the need to please everyone and have everyone like you and approve of you. Of course this is impossible, so you find yourself revising your conversations and actions in order to find the magic key to open the door to everyone's happy place, thereby earning their approval and good opinion of you. You may recognize that this is an irrational, unobtainable goal, and you may even tell yourself that you have to stop thinking this way, but when the guilt sets in, you fall back into the old habits of trying to please and 'make it all ok'.

At its extreme, this kind of guilt can completely immobilize you. You can become so overwhelmed by the fear of doing something 'wrong' or acting in the 'wrong' way or saying the 'wrong' thing that you eventually give up altogether and collapse into a state of inactivity or silence. Rather than saying something that may make someone else uncomfortable (even if it's true), you say nothing or else you agree with whatever is said to you. I have known people who agree with everything, even when having a conversation with two people who are presenting opposite viewpoints. Trying to agree with both at the same time sets up an unbearable tension in the guilt-ridden individual who then tries everything in her power to end the conversation altogether or at least direct the conversation to something everyone can agree on.

Guilt in relationships

The causes of guilt in our relationships with our parents are numerous. It is a well-documented phenomenon that when parents don't get along, when there is fighting in the home, and when divorce happens, children feel guilty. They have the nagging feeling that they are the cause of the conflict or that they could have prevented it. *If only I'd been a better kid, did better in school, kept my room clean, fed the dog, etc., this wouldn't have happened.* Counselors spend thousands of hours convincing children that they are not responsible for their parents' divorce. They didn't cause it and couldn't have prevented it. But still the guilt lingers, often for decades.

As our parents begin to age, we may feel an unexplainable sense of guilt because of our inability to stop this natural process. We see them deteriorating, mentally and physically, before our eyes and we are powerless to stop it. Then the self-accusations begin: *Why didn't I do more/spend more time with them when they were younger? Why did I allow them to do so much for me and spend so much of their energy on me? Why don't I spend more time with them now? I'm just a bad daughter.* We may see our parents slipping away from us into 'the long goodbye' of Alzheimer's, dementia, or just diminished capacity and, for some reason, that produces painful bouts of guilt because we are unable to prevent it. Guilt helps to relieve the sorrow and grief that is a natural part of watching parents age.

Parents often bear heavy burdens of guilt about their children's failures and hardships. If the child shows no interest in God and rebels against going to church, parents (especially mothers) analyze their own behaviors to find the cause. *He is just copying me. I don't always want to go to church. I don't always read the Bible and pray. How can I expect him to want to do those things? It's all my fault.* If he doesn't do well in school, the guilty mother searches for the reasons in her life that are the cause. *I was never good in school. I didn't read to him enough. I let him spend too much time on the computer. It's my fault he's failing.* The fact that he might just be a lazy kid or just has no interest in books or formal learning doesn't occur to the guilty mom. In her mind, she is the cause of all his problems and all his shortcomings can be traced to her.

The guilt-ridden wife whose marriage is in trouble looks to herself for the blame. *I'm a bad wife. I'm not a good enough cook or housekeeper. I'm not attractive enough for him. Look at me! I've gained weight and my face is starting to show age lines. Of course he doesn't love me anymore. Why should he? I don't deserve to be loved anyway.* The shame and self-hatred that guilt often brings are intimacy killers, refusing to allow either love or pleasure. Guilt doesn't allow the wife to trust her husband's positive efforts because she feels she is unworthy of affection. Therefore, all overtures of caring are rejected as illegitimate. *He can't really mean it. He's just pretending.* At its extreme, such guilt becomes paranoia.

The unreasonably guilty woman is often one who feels responsible for her own siblings, especially if they all grew up in the same unhappy home. When little brother Billy decides to be a 'bum', won't work, runs up thousands in credit card debt, and needs a place to crash and play video games all day, Sis willingly gives up the guest room or the basement. She feels she is somehow responsible for the mess he has made of his life, although she can't specifically say why. So to ease her feelings of guilt, she becomes his chief enabler. Not only is this destructive to her own family, straining her relationship with her husband, but it doesn't do Billy any good either. He continues on his path to ruin, shows little or no gratitude to his sister for all she's done for him, and when her husband finally puts his foot down and throws him out, Billy blames her for failing him somehow. Naturally, she feels guilty all over again.

Billy is a perfect example of the kind of person the guilty personality attracts — those who use your guilt to manipulate and control you. Unreasonably guilty women are magnets for the master manipulator. I knew a very attractive young woman who had relationships with one control freak after another. They always appeared to need her help in some way and her naturally tender personality, coupled with a heavy dose of free-floating guilt, put her on the radar screen of many controlling males. Long after she knew she must remove them from her life, she continued in the relationships because breaking up with them made her feel too guilty. Of course whenever she tried to express the need to end it, they manipulated her guilt just enough to make her hesitate. Then the whole dreary process started over. Staying with the guy after she had lost all feeling for him made her feel guilty, but ending the relationship did the same thing. She was caught between two equally distasteful sources of guilt with no way out. As humorist Erma Bombeck so wisely put it: 'Guilt is the gift that keeps on giving.'

Unreasonable guilt can even reach to the rest of the world. You can become convinced that people are starving in Africa because you haven't done something about providing food for them. Some unscrupulous evangelists have convinced guilty Christians that people are sliding into hell because they haven't given enough money, prayed enough, or cared enough. I remember hearing a missionary say to a congregation that we would be held accountable for those who went to hell if we didn't do enough to reach them. Even though I was very young and immature in the faith, something about that statement just didn't seem to ring true. *If I have to take the blame for someone going to hell*, I reasoned, *then I should be able to take credit for someone going to heaven and I know that's not true.* But then again, I never suffered from an overactive sense of guilt, so my reasoning powers overrode any possible feelings of unreasonable guilt.

But existential guilt is powerful enough to override our natural reasoning abilities and cause us to come to conclusions about ourselves, others, life in general and God that are negative, irrational and unbiblical. Feelings, as we have already noted, may or may not be associated with truth and reality. In the case of existential guilt, this is especially so. Therefore, it is crucial that the guilt sufferer applies the principles outlined in chapter 4. The emotion of guilt is so strong and so destructive that it can direct our thinking, instead of the other way around. We simply have to begin by reasoning from truth, not feelings, and allow what we know about truth to rein in our emotions. We *must* be able to say to our guilt, 'You are lying to me. I know the truth.'

No condemnation

Of course the lies and accusations come from the enemy of our souls, he who is the 'accuser of our brothers [and sisters]' (Rev. 12:10) and the father of lies (John 8:44). Of course his goal is to incapacitate us and drive us inward to obsess about ourselves. The last thing he wants is strong, confident women who use objective truth to reject the lies about our subjective feelings of guilt and embrace the truth that will set us free (John 8:32). Make no mistake about the source of unreasonable guilt. It is the enemy of your soul. Nicholas Rowe, eighteenth-century English poet, wrote this about guilt:

> *Guilt is the source of sorrow, 'tis the fiend, the avenging fiend*
> *that follows us behind with whips and stings.*

Imagine the fiend Satan driving you from behind, whipping and stinging you with his endless guilt-producing accusations, until you give up in despair. Then after you've given up, he pursues you with more finger-pointing: *So you've given up, huh? And you call yourself a Christian?*

But he is no match for the truths of the Scripture, the very words of God written down to bring us joy and comfort. I am absolutely convinced that the most important biblical truth that will set the guilt-ridden free is found in Romans 8:1: 'There is now no condemnation for those who are in Christ Jesus.' If there was ever an appropriate life verse for the perpetually guilt-ridden, this is it. So important is this concept that it deserves a thorough examination.

The word 'now' refers to our position as believers in Jesus Christ, we who have come to him in repentance and received him as Savior. There was plenty of condemnation *before*, but there is no condemnation *now*. Now that we belong to him, now that he has taken our sin upon himself on the cross, we are new creations in him. What went before is dead and gone. The 'now' Paul refers to in Romans 8 follows the 'then' he describes in Romans 7, where he argues that because of grace, we are no longer under the law. We are not saved by work of the law, but by grace. We are now dead to the law's penalty and condemnation (Rom. 7:4). So far, so good. Most Christians would agree that they are not trying to live by the Old Testament law. But what about the 'laws' we set upon ourselves? Or those others set for us? These, too, are no longer cause for legitimate condemnation. In other words, there is no basis for us to condemn ourselves, nor is there any basis for anyone else to condemn us. If others set unreasonable demands upon us — or if we set them on ourselves — and we fail, there is still no basis for us to condemn ourselves. There is no criticism that can stick to us, no attack on us that can stand, no reproach, no blame because *now* we are in Christ Jesus.

We cannot be condemned because there is nothing in us — the women we now are in Christ—that is deserving of condemnation. We are beyond the reach of any kind of legitimate censure. That doesn't mean we are perfect and sinless, nor will we ever be until we reach heaven. But God doesn't see us as needing punishment for anything we do or say. He has already pardoned us for those things, not because we deserved to be pardoned, but because he has determined to pardon us for the sake of his own glory and name. Over and over in the Old Testament, God held back his hand from punishing the Israelites when they rejected him. He says many times that he showed mercy on them, not because they earned it or deserved it, but for his 'name's sake'. He did it to show the benevolence of his character and to promote his glory among the nations. He did it for *his* sake, not theirs. So when we fail, he continues to love and forgive us because it is his nature to do so and he is glorified by expressing that nature. 'If we are faithless, he will remain faithful, for [because] he cannot disown himself' (2 Tim. 2:13).

Imagine you have committed a crime worthy of the death penalty and you are in prison awaiting execution, along with other Death Row inmates. One day the warden comes by, opens your cell, and says, 'You are free to go.'When you ask why, he tells you that he is a merciful, kind, gracious person who has decided to free you for no other reason than to express his mercy, kindness and grace. 'But I am guilty!' you cry. 'But I am merciful,' he replies. Would you draw back into your cell and pull the door closed? Of course not. You would run for the door.

So it is with God. He pardoned us to express his own nature, his own grace and mercy so that in that expression, he is glorified, praised and worshiped. You are not the cause of his mercy, you did nothing to deserve or merit it. You are merely the recipient of his gracious and abundant love. To hold on to the guilt and remorse you feel is to reject the gift of God's mercy. It is the same as the prisoner who refuses the pardon and sits in his stinking cell looking forward to his execution. It may seem that it is impossible to accept this free gift, but if you are 'in Christ Jesus', *you have already accepted it.* All that needs to happen now is to realize what that means and be able to distinguish between the lies your guilt is telling you and the glorious truths that God is telling you.

Examining the lies

Let's look at some of those lies in light of Romans 8:1: *I am unhappy, but that's ok because I don't deserve to be happy.* I have news for you. No one deserves to be happy. That's the beauty of the incarnation. Jesus came to bring peace and joy to those who do not deserve it — you, me, and all who belong to him. He enables us to have this incredible joy, even though we are undeserving of this wondrous gift. He brought forgiveness of sin, not condemnation. On the cross, he exchanged our unrighteous natures for his own perfect righteousness (2 Cor. 5:17), crucifying our sin nature and burying it in the tomb. We died with him and were resurrected with him to 'walk in newness of life' (Rom. 6:4, NKJV). Did you get that? The old 'you' is dead. Not just mortally wounded. Dead. You can't be condemned because there is nothing to condemn. Jesus was condemned for you. There is now *no condemnation* for you because you are in Christ. Oh, that we could only grasp this marvelous truth!

Another lie: *If I feel this guilty, I must have something to be guilty about.* So you spend endless hours of mental and emotional energy trying to determine what it is that causes your nagging guilt. Guilt is a feeling, an emotion, and as such it is the opposite of rational thought based on truth. The false idea that we have to *feel* forgiven in order to be so is common. This is the 'emotion determining truth' paradigm we talked about in chapter 4. It goes like this: 'I still *feel* guilty so therefore I must *be* guilty,' instead of 'God has declared me to be forgiven and Christ gave his life for me. Therefore, I *am* forgiven, *no matter how I feel*, and there is no condemnation that can be applied to me.' Truth should drive feelings, instead of the other way around. Feelings are not the issue; truth is the issue. What you feel is not the determiner of reality or of truth.

A third lie: *God can't possibly love me because I'm too _____*. (Fill in the blank with whatever you're feeling guilty about.) Once again, the issue here is not whether you are worthy of God's love. You're not. No one is. He loves us, not because we are worthy of his love, but because he determined to set his love upon us before he even created the world. His plan was to choose us, according to his will, 'in order that we, who were the first to hope in Christ, might be for the praise of his glory' (Eph. 1:12). Do we understand that? For *his* glory. For *his* name's sake. To display *his* glory. For *his* praise. We didn't cause him to love us and we don't have to do anything to continue to be loved by him. He will always love us because that is who he is and what he has purposed to do. And one of the things he has determined to do is *not* to condemn his children!

The power source

So how do we deal with these feelings of guilt? As I was doing research for this chapter, I was amazed at the number of recommendations by psychologists that involved self-effort and self-reformation. If fixing this problem were simply a matter of making a decision to stop feeling guilty or determining to take control of the mind, no one would ever suffer from existential guilt. In fact, it wouldn't even exist because it could be so easily dispensed with. But it does exist and the guilt-ridden person is unable to free herself from it. She is in a prison cell and the key is beyond her reach. What else does the secular world have to offer except the power of the self? But the woman without the Holy Spirit is simply incapable of fixing herself. She is as powerless as Donna parked in that lonely field in the blizzard. But as Christians, we have a completely different solution, one that actually works because it doesn't rely on our own power. Rather, it draws on the power of the Holy Spirit who lives in our hearts. Just as the strong arms of those soldiers lifted Donna from her car, so the Spirit's power lifts us up to higher ground where there is peace and joy.

One thing is for sure. Obsessing about the guilt never gets rid of the guilt. Thinking, *'How can I relieve the guilt I feel?'* or *'Why do I feel guilty?'* keeps our minds on the guilt instead of on God and his forgiveness of our sin, his perfect will and determination to love us, the power of the Holy Spirit who lives in us, and the reality of the Savior's sacrifice which enables us to say, 'I can do all things through Christ who strengthens me' (Phil. 4:13, NKJV). The same applies to doubt, fear, and all other negative emotions. Obsessing about any feeling, whether positive or negative, is self-obsession and it comes from being unsure of the forgiveness and nature of God. This self-obsession is part of the sin nature, the part that Satan influences.

After Paul assures us that there is now no condemnation for those in Christ, he goes on to tell us how to break the power of the sin nature we still have to deal with, the part of us that Satan manipulates to accuse us and make us feel guilty, in spite of having been made 'new creations in Christ' (2 Cor. 5:17). Paul declares in the rest of Romans 8 some truths for us to hang onto. 'The mind of sinful man is death, but the mind controlled by the Spirit is life and peace' (Rom. 8:6). A mind controlled by the Spirit seeks those feelings which the Holy Spirit produces — love, joy, peace and the other fruits of the Spirit (Gal. 5:22). As Christians, we all have the Spirit within us but we 'quench the Spirit' (1 Thess. 5:19, NKJV) by not feeding our hearts and minds with the things that enlarge his influence in our lives.

When we neglect the spiritual disciplines of prayer, Bible study, and attending a church that accurately and diligently preaches and teaches the Word of God, we quench the Spirit. When we allow vanity, ambition, pride, or the indulging of sensuality to replace purity and godliness, we quench the Spirit. The Spirit within us is like water that flows down from the mountain. When we neglect the things of the Spirit and feed our sin nature, the Spirit's influence in our lives is like a small trickle of water, a tiny stream. But when we feed the Spirit with the things of the Spirit, his influence becomes a huge raging torrent rushing downhill, demolishing barriers and carrying everything before its tremendous power. Puny little feelings of guilt are no match for the unleashed power of the Spirit of God.

Will those irrational feelings of guilt go away completely? For many women, the answer is no. They will still rise up and try to control us. But when the timeless truths of God saturate our hearts and minds, we can identify the lie that we have something to be guilty about and respond to it with truth. *God has told me that he has removed my sin 'as far as the east is from the west'* (Ps. 103:12). *Therefore, I know this feeling of guilt is a lie.* When our guilt rises up and accuses us of being less than we should be, we can respond with *I may be a weakling, but Jesus has promised to* keep me *'strong to the end, so that [I] will be blameless on the day of our Lord Jesus Christ'* (1 Cor. 1:8). When our consciences plague us with thoughts of our failures, and we feel compelled to *do something* to relieve it, we can answer with 'How much more shall the blood of Christ, who through the eternal Spirit offered himself without spot to God, cleanse your conscience from dead works to serve the living God?' (Heb. 9:14, NKJV). Then we can rest from the 'dead works' that are of no value and serve God in the joy of the new life he provides for us.

These and many other promises of God, when they are anchored in your heart, will untangle the knot of guilt and remorse that keeps you from experiencing the peace that 'passes all understanding' (Phil. 4:7, NKJV) and your joy will be full. God has promised it.

8

So mad I could spit!:

Anger

We live in an increasingly angry world. Perhaps that is a sign that the end of the age is upon us. From the mobs in the Arab street to the thugs knocking over the local liquor store, anger is everywhere. It seems that just about everyone is in a temper about something. Those who protest against the government are seething with resentment and, oddly enough, no matter what the government does, someone is angry about it. The more laws and regulations that are passed, the more the 'less government control' crowd get angry. But there are always those who want more and more from the government and when they don't get it, they explode into the streets demanding their 'rights' to free health care, free lunches in schools, free transportation, free everything. The unions are mad at business and business owners are mad at the IRS and other government agencies.

Liberals and conservatives snipe at each other over the talk radio airwaves. Democrats and Republicans blame each other for the mess the country is in, although whether it's actually in a mess or not is often not even relevant, as long as the electorate is sufficiently outraged. What is worse, we seem to enjoy expressions of anger. TV programs and movies that are filled with explosions, gunfire, violence, murder and mayhem are more popular than ever. And more and more people feel the need to carry guns to protect themselves from angry criminals. Gun sales are at an all-time high, even while anti-gun lobbies, incensed at those who would dare to own and carry firearms, try to legislate away the Second Amendment.

On the personal level, it seems everyone has someone in his/ her life to vent their anger upon, whether or not it's deserved. A simple mistake by a motorist can be life-threatening and road rage can erupt over the most innocent act. Somehow the angry motorist has convinced himself that his part of the road is truly his and woe to the 'idiot' who dares to infringe upon it. Husbands and wives are mad at each other so often that everything from the 'silent treatment' to spousal abuse is prevalent in too many homes. Children are mad at each other and take out their aggression on both friends and siblings. Teenagers are mad at parents, and parents are mad at teachers and principals, all of whom in turn vent their anger at the school boards.

Then there are those who are just mad at the world. They are all over the internet, spewing their vitriol in profane posts in the blogosphere, ranting and raving in videos on YouTube, and creating violent and threatening web sites where they can vent their spleens on the rest of us. Hollywood has homed in on all this fury, giving us a plethora of 'reality' TV shows with angry people, mostly women, acting like raging bulls bent on mayhem and destruction. Portraying everything from monster brides to out-of-control mothers of child beauty queens, these shows inevitably feature women screaming and swearing at one another. What all these people have in common is a seething hatred for anyone and anything that has in some way offended them, disrespected them, or restricted their freedom to do exactly as they please, whenever and however they see fit. The two teens who massacred thirteen people in Colorado at Columbine High School in 1999 had made clear not only their wrath, but their intention to get revenge on those who were perceived as having slighted them. The fact that they hardly knew most of their victims was irrelevant. They were boiling over with rage and someone was going to pay with their lives.

The first angry man

Just as murderous fury was the cause of the Columbine tragedy, the very first murder was also the result of rage. Cain killed his brother, Abel, because God was pleased with Abel's offering, but 'did not look with favor' on Cain or his offering. Hebrews 11:4 clarifies, saying that Abel's offering was 'by faith' whereas Cain's 'actions were evil' (1 John 3:12). Evil always displeases the Lord, but instead of repenting and offering an acceptable sacrifice, 'Cain was very angry, and his face was downcast' (Gen. 4:5). His anger led to murder.

The Hebrew word translated 'angry' here gives a poignant description of the emotion of anger: *to glow or grow warm; to blaze up in anger, zeal, or jealousy.* Anger affects the body and the face in just this way. Social commentator Henry Fairlie, in his book *The Seven Deadly Sins Today,* describes it perfectly:

We think of Anger in terms of fire: blazing, flaming, scorching, smoking, fuming, spitting, smoldering, heated, white hot, simmering, boiling, and even when it is ice-cold it will still burn. It has been called the Devil's furnace, and other sins will fuel it.

Clearly Cain's anger was ignited and honed in Satan's furnace, and people have been murdering one another ever since.

The reference to ice-cold anger reveals another aspect of fury, that which simmers and stews, plotting revenge until it has the opportunity to explode in a frenzy of violence, whether physical or verbal. An old proverb, 'Revenge is a dish best served cold', is certainly fitting to those who allow their anger to fester. The angry person's ire can be contained and controlled for days or even years, but eventually it will have its way. Who knows how long it was after Cain was rebuked by God that he lured his brother into a field and killed him? It could have been hours, days, or weeks. How long did Cain fester and simmer, blaming his failure on his innocent brother and working himself up into a murderous rage? However long it takes, once anger is let loose, it will always have its day of vengeance.

There are two situations in which anger is justifiable — when defending God or defending the innocent. Jesus displayed righteous, justified anger both times he cleansed the temple of those who had turned his Father's house into a den of thieves. Unscrupulous money-changers were charging exorbitant fees to change the Roman coins currently in use to the Jewish half-shekel required for the sacrifice. Sellers of birds and animals for the required sacrifices were also overcharging the poor who had no animals of their own to sacrifice. When Jesus made a whip of cords and angrily drove out the ungodly merchants, he was both purifying his Father's house and protecting the innocent from their abuse (Matt. 21:12-13; John 2:13-17).

When we become angry with those who lie and distort the doctrines of the faith, leading others into hell and bringing reproach on the name of Christ, our anger is justified. When we see innocent children, the poor, weak and helpless being abused or taken advantage of, our anger is justified. All Christians should abhor evil in all its forms, but especially evil directed against the nature of God or the innocent. Even justifiable anger, however, must be short-lived. Even righteous anger can turn to bitterness and hostility against others if allowed to fester, which is why Paul commands us to 'not let the sun go down while you are still angry' (Eph. 4:26).

The root causes of anger

Clearly, many hearts are tangled and strangled by anger, rage, fury, wrath and fits of temper. But why? Why are so many people harboring so much anger? Why are so many acting out their anger in so many ways? Why are so many people turning their anger inward and living with unexpressed bitterness and simmering resentment? Worse, why are so many turning their anger outward upon others, often innocent strangers? Why is everyone mad at everyone else? Is this normal? And, as Christian women, how do we regard our anger and what do we do about it?

Some of our anger may be left over from childhood. I remember being a very angry kid, frequently given to outbursts of rage. At the time, I attributed it to my 'Irish temper', but as I matured, I realized that living in a home where there was constant turmoil between my parents, along with some merciless teasing by an older brother, had left me with a great deal of anger. For years, I vented my anger on others, usually in the form of verbal 'put-downs'. As Christ came into my life and began to recreate me in his image, I came to realize that James was right when he described the tongue as 'a fire, a world of evil among the parts of the body' and when he said that 'anger does not bring about the righteous life that God desires' (James 3:6; 1:20). But the scars of childhood can last for years, which is why God commands fathers not to provoke their children to anger (Eph. 6:4, ESV) or 'embitter' their children (Col. 3:21). Such provocation can lead to drastic consequences. The tragic 1989 case of the Menendez brothers who killed their parents with shotguns in their Beverly Hills mansion is an example. Whether their father abused them emotionally or sexually, or both, clearly he provoked and embittered them to the point that shooting their parents point blank was, in their minds, justified.

Who has not seen a toddler fly into a fit of rage when he doesn't get what he wants, when he wants it? This is the uncontrolled anger typical of children who have not yet developed the ability to restrain it. They react to being oppressed or frustrated in the only way they can, spewing the emotion of anger all over everyone. But as we mature, anger involves more than an emotional reaction. It involves both the reason and the will. We make a conscious choice to let loose our anger. This is sin — anger unleashed knowingly and willingly.

Just like the toddler who can't have his way, anger is often produced when we don't get something which we believe we deserve to have. What we believe we deserve can be anything from material goods to the respect and appreciation of others. Who hasn't seen professional athletes get into fights because they felt they were disrespected by opposing players or even fans? The man who doesn't get the promotion he has worked for is angry with his boss. The wife whose husband neglects to fulfill her needs simmers until the time to 'get even' presents itself. Then she makes her displeasure known in a variety of ways, from screaming at him to the silent treatment or withholding sex. In all these cases, the anger comes from not being perceived by others in the way we perceive ourselves. The athlete sees himself as worthy of praise, not disrespect. The working man perceives himself as more worthy of a bigger paycheck and the wife perceives herself as worthy of her husband's undivided attention. The problem is that if we think we have legitimate cause to be angry, we convince ourselves we can act from anger in whatever way we please, and any amount of destructive behavior then becomes justified. This is nothing more than pride running rampant; and pride, as the Scripture tells us, goes before destruction (Prov. 16:18).

Nothing is more destructive than uncontrolled anger. Despite the modern psychologists' claims that anger can be used constructively, the book of Proverbs tells us that those who give full rein to their anger are fools. 'A fool shows his annoyance at once, but a prudent man overlooks an insult' (Prov. 12:16). The foolish woman who shows her annoyance is one who cannot repress it or rein it in. It shows in her face, in her fiery eyes and her poison tongue spewing venom on her annoyers. Woe to the husband or child who is in the line of fire. I once knew a woman whose volatile temper was well known to her friends and family. When Darlene was irritated, everyone dived for cover. How sad that she didn't understand anger is both self-destructive and the destroyer of relationships.

Darlene's acquaintances often avoided her because her fits of temper were unpredictable and her anger never far below the surface. Like a volcano, she could erupt at any moment and with the least provocation. Her friends began to back away from her, heeding the proverb, 'Do not make friends with a hot-tempered man [or woman], do not associate with one easily angered, or you may learn his ways and get yourself ensnared' (Prov. 22:24-25). Even if they weren't afraid of being 'ensnared', who wants to have to walk around on eggshells with someone who may explode at any moment? Darlene's temper was a detriment to her marriage as well, and her husband must have read Proverbs 21:19 with a sad nod of agreement: 'Better to dwell in the wilderness, than with a contentious and angry woman' (NKJV).

Nothing good comes from anger. It is self-destructive. It destroys relationships. It is deadly to a marriage. The Bible is clear on all these results of harboring anger. Why, then, do people, even Christians, want to hold onto their anger? In some cases, it is a defense mechanism. Presenting an angry front to the world helps to insulate us from the hurts that are inevitable living in a world with other fallen human beings. It's easier to put people off with an angry word or stony look than to be vulnerable to them. But this leads to isolation and loneliness, which can lead to more anger. Isn't it better to heed what God says about anger? 'Refrain from anger and turn from wrath; do not fret — it leads only to evil' (Ps. 37:8). To 'fret' in the Hebrew means to burn and simmer in anger, and as we have seen, all kinds of evil result from it, both to the angry one and those around her. 'An angry man [or woman] stirs up dissension, and a hot-tempered one commits many sins' (Prov. 29:22). Those 'many sins' can be anything from unkindness to murder and everything in between.

God knows how difficult it can be to live in a fallen world, especially for those who are sensitive and easily hurt. But that is no excuse for anger and the angry person will not escape the consequences. Proverbs 19:19 says, 'A hot-tempered man [or woman] must pay the penalty.' The penalties for angry behavior are numerous and inevitable. Parents who chastise their children out of anger will find their children returning the favor, especially in the teen years. The woman who gives way to wrath toward her husband creates a marriage characterized by continual quarreling and a lack of love. Uncontrolled anger can lead to dire acts that inevitably bring punishment from the legal system. And if all these potential consequences are not enough to deter the angry person, there is the inevitable displeasure of a God who will not allow his children to continue in sinful behaviors but will discipline them in his own righteous anger.

Jesus also reminds us that anger and bitterness can lead to murder. 'You have heard that it was said to the people long ago, "Do not murder, and anyone who murders will be subject to judgement." But I tell you that anyone who is angry with his brother will be subject to judgement' (Matt. 5:21-22). Would Cain have murdered Abel if he hadn't been angry? What about the Columbine killers or the Menendez brothers? Jesus is warning against anger because anger is never satisfied until it has its revenge.

There's just no way around the fact that anger is sin and the angry person commits many sins. Anger can lead to bitterness, violence and even murder. There is just no 'up side' to harboring anger within our hearts, no matter the cause and no matter how much we feel we have been abused or disrespected. For the Christian woman, there is the added sorrow of having grieved the Lord who saved her, died for her, and loves her.

Anger and the fruit of the Spirit

For the Christian woman, anger is the most damaging of all negative emotions. We have already seen that anger destroys marriages and other relationships, as well as being self-destructive. But this is equally true of angry non-believers. What distinguishes a Christian from a non-Christian is the presence of the Holy Spirit in her heart. As we've said before, the Spirit doesn't come into the life of a believer and then sit there for the rest of her life doing nothing. He *will* produce fruit. And of the different fruit he produces, not one is compatible with anger. In fact, each of the fruits of the Spirit described in Galatians 5:22-23 is the exact opposite of anger: 'But the fruit of the Spirit is love, joy, peace, patience, kindness, goodness, faithfulness, gentleness and self-control.' None of these fruits can characterize the life of a Christian when anger and wrath are also present. They are mutually exclusive.

The 'love' the Spirit produces is *agape* love, the love which comes from God. The *agape* lover is not the sighing, fainting, sentimental lover who gushes and burbles and coos all over everyone. The woman with the Spirit's love in her heart sacrifices for others and puts others' concerns and needs before her own, just as Jesus put the needs of others ahead of his own and went to the cross to fulfil our greatest need — forgiveness of sin. The woman who is frequently in a rage loves no one but herself, and she gives free rein to her anger because she feels entitled to do so. The angry woman loves the expression of her wrath. She loves the feeling of release it gives her and the control it gives her over others. She loves herself more than others and she indulges her own need to blow her top.

It goes without saying that the angry woman cannot be joyful. The Greek word translated 'joy' in Galatians 5 means literally 'cheerfulness and calm delight'. The woman in a temper is not cheerful, calm or delightful. Her face and voice betray her ire, and even when she tries to cover it up with a religious exterior, those who know her understand that she is a ticking time-bomb. Not only does she not have joy in her own heart, but her effect on those close to her is to rob them of joy as well.

When Jesus died on the cross for us, he obtained for us peace with God (Rom. 5:1). No longer fearful of punishment for sin, the effect of the peace Jesus purchased for us is a quietness and tranquility of mind. Since we have peace with God and the peace of mind that faith in him produces, we also have peace with others, Christians and non-Christians alike. We seek after the things that make for peace, and we desire to live peaceably with all others. The angry woman has no peace. Hers is not a peaceful heart, but one tangled and strangled with out-of-control rages.

Patience is another spiritual fruit that cannot co-exist with anger. The KJV word for patience is 'longsuffering', an attribute of God. He is 'longsuffering' with us, withholding his righteous anger and patiently waiting for his children to come to repentance. Because of his patience toward us, his children are to be 'completely humble and gentle; … patient, bearing with one another in love' (Eph. 4:2). What characterizes the angry woman is her inability to bear with others in love. Others irritate her. They annoy her. They disappoint her. She has no patience with them, although she expects them to be patient with her while she displays her displeasure with outbursts of temper.

The Greek words for kindness, goodness and gentleness in the New Testament are often used interchangeably. All carry with them the idea of graciousness and kindness of heart, exhibited in words and action. The heart filled with wrath is not capable of kind words or gracious acts. The angry woman may be continually busy with good works — providing meals, serving in the nursery, visiting hospitals — but her heart isn't in it. In truth, she hates what she is doing because she does it out of obligation, not out of love for God and his people. Her acts of 'charity' are not charitable at all; they are dreary duties performed by an unwilling heart. Even when she forces herself to use kind words and gracious speech, her eyes often betray her and reveal a heart simmering with anger. Not only does this hypocrisy displease God, but it further increases her anger. And so it goes, on and on and on.

The spiritual fruit of faithfulness does not refer to the gift of faith which is given to all believers (Eph. 2:8-9). Rather, faithfulness means trustworthiness and reliability, and it is another of God's attributes. When we are filled with the Spirit and walking in obedience to God, others trust us. They know our words are reliable. They can count on us to 'walk the walk' of faith. But those around the angry woman can only rely on her being unpredictable in her behavior. She is faithful only to her own wrath and her need to 'blow up' regularly, either to maintain what she sees as control or to intimidate others into behaving in a way she finds acceptable. Those who are close to the wrathful woman can only count on her anger, not her faith or her faithfulness. In fact, in all she does, she contradicts her Christian testimony.

The last of the spiritual fruits mentioned in Galatians 5 is self-control. It is obvious that the angry woman has no control over her rage. Self-control is the mastery of all our evil tendencies. It can refer to anything from avoiding intoxicating drinks and overeating to control of all kinds of passions, including sexual. The angry woman's tendency is to vent her inward rages, to blow like a volcano spewing verbal lava on the surrounding territory. She exhibits none of the influences of the Holy Spirit on her heart, those which would curb her self-indulgence and enable her to restrain her passions and to govern herself.

Getting real with anger

The foregoing may seem to be a harsh indictment against women with anger issues, especially those who believe their anger is justified or whose anger has its root cause in abuse of some kind. Of course true believers have moments when they give in to anger. But the woman whose anger characterizes her life and who sees no reason to seek forgiveness for it has cause to wonder if the Spirit may be absent from her life, especially if she secretly enjoys her anger and the control over others her anger often generates. Anger is no greater sin than any other, and like all sin, it can be identified as such and repented of. Holding on to anger, whatever its source, is self-destructive, stunts spiritual growth, and grieves the heart of God.

When the Spirit of God comes into the heart at the moment of salvation, he begins the process of changing behavior to line up with the new person Christ has created. Yes, we still sin, but we hate our sin and we desire to be rid of it. We don't wallow in it and enjoy its power. Our new nature convicts us of sin, prompts us to long for something better, and drives us to ask for the Spirit's power to change our behavior. In the same passage where we find the fruit of the Spirit, Paul describes the difference between the old, sinful nature and the new nature in Christ: 'For the sinful nature desires what is contrary to the Spirit, and the Spirit what is contrary to the sinful nature. They are in conflict with each other, so that *you do not do what you want*' (Gal. 5:17, emphasis added). We may still have moments of anger, but it's not what we desire to do.

Anger may be evidence that the old sinful nature is still in control or may testify to the unchanged state of the heart. 'The acts of the sinful nature are obvious: sexual immorality, impurity and debauchery; idolatry and witchcraft; hatred, discord, jealousy, *fits of rage*, selfish ambition, dissensions, factions and envy; drunkenness, orgies, and the like. I warn you, as I did before, that *those who live like this* will not inherit the kingdom of God' (Gal. 5:19-21, emphasis added). Here, sadly, is the crux of the matter — the woman given to fits of rage, outbursts of uncontrolled anger, especially if she inwardly enjoys them, is evidencing a lack of the Spirit in her life. Paul makes that very clear when he says that those who 'live like this will not inherit the kingdom of God'. All believers inherit the kingdom of God, so those whom he describes in this passage are clearly not believers.

John affirms this by describing those who belong to Christ: 'No one who lives in him keeps on sinning. No one who continues to sin has either seen him or known him' (1 John 3:6). To 'keep on sinning' in the case of anger is to justify it in some way, to desire to cling to it, or to enjoy its power. There is just no way around the fact that the perpetually angry woman is living a sinful lifestyle. She may have made a profession of faith or prayed the prayer of salvation, but does she truly 'abide' with Christ and he with her? Does she show evidence of the love and affection for him which produce obedience and sorrow when she grieves him with her sin of anger? These are questions she must ask herself.

This is why the first step in untangling hearts is to make our calling and election sure. The unsaved woman has no power to control her anger, no desire to be rid of it once and for all, and no hope for the future. But fortunately, her anger can be a wake-up call to examine herself to see if she is truly in the faith. If what she sees in her examination leads her to the conclusion that she simply cannot be a child of God, the cure is to fall to her knees at the foot of Jesus and ask him to forgive her sins and come into her life and heart. The joyful truth is that he will *always* forgive and accept anyone who comes to him in sincerity, no matter how grievous the sin and no matter how long the sinful lifestyle has continued. There is no pit so deep, no darkness so overwhelming, that the love of Christ cannot penetrate it.

Once saved, the Christian woman often makes the mistake of assuming she can conquer all sinful tendencies by the sheer force of her will or by making resolutions or using three-step plans so commonly offered up by the self-help gurus. The fact is that we have no power of our own to conquer anger. Just like Donna stuck in her car in the blizzard, we have to be rescued by the strong arms of the Spirit of God, the only one who can conquer sin in our lives. Striving to not be angry won't work.

Praying to the Spirit to exert his power over our anger will. Obsessing about our anger and other sins won't work either. Obsessing about God is the only way to clear the mind of sinful thoughts and remove sinful tendencies from the heart. God has promised that those whose minds are fixed on him will have perfect peace (Isa. 26:3).

A word to those whose anger stems from past abuses: the only way to have peace with your past is by the power of the Spirit who alone can turn your anger against your abuser to sorrow over their destiny — an eternity in hell. Only God can produce a true spirit of forgiveness in your heart. So ask him to do that. As you yield more and more to him, as you learn more about him and experience his kindness toward you, your outrage toward others will fade and you will find that 'the peace of God, which transcends all understanding, will guard your hearts and your minds in Christ Jesus' (Phil. 4:7).

In the third chapter of Paul's letter to the Colossians, verses 1-10 outline the thrilling truths of the power of God at work in our lives when we belong to him. Having been 'raised with Christ', we are now to set our hearts and minds 'on things above, not on earthly things' (vv. 1-2). When our hearts are filled with God's truth and our minds are continually on him, anger loses its power over us, not because we are working hard to get rid of it, but because it simply pales in comparison to our new focus. The Christian woman who is overwhelmed by the love of God for her, and in her, will find the appeal and control of anger diminish and eventually fade away. It is just no match for the love of Christ and the power of the Holy Spirit in her heart.

9

I'll never get over it:

Bitterness

In the US in the 1990s, Budweiser aired a series of commercials during the Super Bowls featuring two disgruntled lizards named Frankie and Louie. The premise was that the pair had failed to win roles in Budweiser commercials, losing out to the now famous Budweiser Frogs. Louie was particularly annoyed by the rejection: 'I can't believe they went with the frogs. Our audition was flawless! We could have been huge! Those frogs … are gonna pay.'

In subsequent commercials, Louie hires a ferret as a hit man who somehow manages to drop the neon Budweiser sign from the swamp bar into the water, electrocuting the frogs. Louie snickers and says, 'Sooner or later, every frog has to croak.' Even when his friend, Frankie, asks incredulously: 'What have you done, Louie?', Louie declares this to be the best day of his life. But when the frogs turn up alive and well, Louie is devastated. Later, he rejoices when he finds out one of the frogs has developed a nervous tic and cannot act anymore.

My favorite line from the commercials is Frankie's advice: 'Let it go, Louie. Let it go.' To this day, my husband and I use that phrase when one of us is rankled about something, reminding each other to 'Let it go, Louie.' But Louie can't let it go. He festers and stews about his loss. His bitterness, although amusing in a commercial, is sadly representative of the bitterness that chokes and tangles the hearts of so many women, even Christian women. Granted, those who suffer the agonies of bitter resentment and regrets don't usually hire a hit man to take out their tormentors, but how many of us would do just that if we could get away with it?! When we are in the grip of bitterness, we just can't seem to 'let it go'.

Closely related to rage, which is anger turned outward, bitterness is anger turned inward. The bitter woman may not vent her anger in verbal, or even physical, outbursts. She doesn't throw the china against the wall or kick the dog. More often, she sits and stews over past offenses, often rehashing every incident where she was hurt, abused or insulted, and every hateful word spoken to her or about her. She may fantasize about avenging herself on those who have offended her, imagining herself withering them with a barrage of well-chosen words that leave them speechless. Worse, she may even conjure up fantasy murders or other heinous crimes. Like Louie, who rejoiced in the idea of electrocuting his rivals, we can allow our bitterness-driven imaginations to run wild.

Is there any more haunting imagery than that evoked by the phrase 'a root of bitterness'? The causes of bitterness are closely related to the causes of anger. The woman with past hurts and abuses who does not show them with outward anger often turns them inwardly, causing that bitter root to grow deeper and deeper, entwining itself around her insides and strangling
120

her heart and mind. Bitterness is the root; anger is the fruit. Bitterness turns inward and rots us from the inside out. Anger is the explosion that results from inward bitterness.

How bitterness develops

The New Testament word translated 'bitterness' means something acrid, especially poison, and so many women poison themselves and all around them with their bitterness, resentment and hostility. Similar to anger in that it devastates relationships, the causes of bitterness are numerous, but there is only one 'cure' — the grace and love and mercy of God in Christ.

A friend who spent more than a year having bitter regrets about the treatment she and her family had received by a church they had attended nailed it on the head when I asked her what she thought was the source of her bitterness. 'Disappointment,' she said, 'from expectations.' How true. Whatever and whoever the bitter woman sees as the reasons for her bitterness, inevitably the underlying cause is that she expected something she felt she deserved and when she didn't get it, the deep disappointment of dashed expectations produced a bitter heart. The woman who was abandoned by her father as a child or who lived with a cold, unloving mother, the wife whose 'Prince Charming' turns out to be more like an ogre, the mother whose children disappoint her by not turning out the way she had planned, the church worker whose efforts seem to go unnoticed and unappreciated — all can find themselves in a perpetual state of bitter resentment.

But bitterness just as often results from regrets over our own failures as from disappointment that stems from our expectations of others. Like Louie, dashed hopes and dreams we had for ourselves can come back to haunt us when we see ourselves as somehow inadequate or powerless to make them come to pass.

The story of Simon the sorcerer in Acts 8 is a perfect example of bitterness due to unfulfilled expectations and desires. Envious that the Spirit was given at the laying on of the hands of Peter and John, he offered them money to obtain this same power (v. 18). Peter's response was a rebuke:

> 'May your money perish with you, because you thought you could buy the gift of God with money! You have no part or share in this ministry, because your heart is not right before God. Repent of this wickedness and pray to the Lord. Perhaps he will forgive you for having such a thought in your heart. For I see that you are full of bitterness and captive to sin'
>
> (Acts 8:20-23).

Peter's assessment of Simon includes the traits of bitterness and bondage to sin. Here are two clear outcomes of bitterness — it both poisons and binds. When bitterness takes root in our hearts, it spreads throughout our lives just as arsenic spreads throughout the body if it is ingested. Like a virus that is transmitted through the air, once it takes up residence in the nose, it quickly spreads throughout the body, producing all the miserable symptoms of a cold or flu. So it is with the root of bitterness. No doubt Simon had at one time a 'root' of bitterness, but it had grown and developed until Peter could see that Simon was *full* of bitterness.

The cause of Simon's bitterness is typical — he wanted something someone else had. Bitterness and envy are closely related and both are caused by the same things: disappointed hopes and unfulfilled desires. Further, instead of being respected for his desire to have the power of the Spirit, as was his expectation, he was rebuked by Peter who could see that his heart was not right before the Lord. His motive for wanting the Spirit's power was self-aggrandizement, not the glory of God and the salvation of others. So often we expect to be lauded and admired for our abilities and accomplishments, but when we are not esteemed in the way we believe we deserve, the root of bitterness begins to form. Then each time our expectations end in disappointment, the root digs itself down a little deeper. Over time, that root becomes huge and it sucks the spiritual life out of us.

Our yard is fairly large and our neighborhood has many mature trees. One day we noticed that one of the sprinkler heads that water the back yard was leaking. My husband replaced the head, but the leak continued. It wasn't until he dug down deeper that he realized the pipeline had been broken by the roots of the neighbor's tree which had spread under the fence into our yard. Roots will always seek sources of water and this particular root wrapped itself around the pipe until it crushed it open, sucking the life-giving water from our sprinkler system. What an appropriate picture of the root of bitterness. It seeks the source of life — the heart — until it drains the life out of it. This is why we are told, 'Above all else, guard your heart, for it is the wellspring of life' (Prov. 4:23).

Simon was full of the poison of bitterness, and along with that poison came its inevitable partner — the bondage of sin. There is no room in the life of a Christian for the sin of bitterness. It is inconsistent with the testimony of the saving grace of God in Christ. It binds and strangles us and holds us in its power.

It is a progression

Paul exhorts the Ephesians to live in such a way as to prove they belong to Christ and not grieve the Holy Spirit. 'Get rid of all bitterness, rage and anger, brawling and slander, along with every form of malice' (Eph. 4:30-31). Notice the progression of the sins in this verse. Bitterness, the inner bondage, leads to rage and anger which produce physical violence (brawling) and verbal violence (slander) toward others. This leads to other forms of 'malice' (evil, wickedness, depravity). No wonder bitterness is described as a root. It strangles the heart just as surely as that tree root strangled the water line, holding the heart captive and producing the fruit of evil.

Tearing up the root

Of course the best way to avoid the poison and bondage of bitterness is to not let it take root to begin with. 'See to it that no one misses the grace of God and that no bitter root grows up to cause trouble and defile many' (Heb. 12:15). But what about the heart tangled and entwined by the bitter root that has grown up over years of disappointments and dashed hopes? How do we tear up that root? First, we have to recognize bitterness for what it is — sin. And we deal with the sin of bitterness in exactly the same way we deal with all sin in our lives. We take it to God and confess it. God is 'faithful and just and will forgive us our sins and purify us from all unrighteousness' (1 John 1:9). Our loving heavenly Father doesn't want us to suffer the torture of bitterness because he knows how much it hurts us. And he knows it keeps us from enjoying his presence and the sense of his love and care for us. He is waiting for us to say, 'This is the wrong way to think and the wrong way to feel. Forgive me and please take away this bitterness. You are the only one who can.'

Once we have admitted that bitterness is sin and understand the necessity of being rid of it if our hearts are to begin untangling, we have to be on guard lest the root of bitterness starts to grow again. Since bitterness is usually caused by disappointments, we have to adjust our expectations. Our expectations of others must be adjusted to the reality of the human heart, the human experience, and the fact of the spiritual battle. Even the best of us, the most spiritual of us, still lives in the fallen flesh, the temporary 'tent' in which we live which causes us to 'groan, being burdened' (2 Cor. 5:4, NKJV). Others fail us. They disillusion us. They thwart our plans and frustrate our desires. That is the nature of living in a sin-cursed world under the control of Satan. The only way to avoid the ugly results of dashed expectations from the failures of other people is to see them as struggling just as we are and to pray for the spirit of forgiveness that only comes from God. After all, he forgave us when we were in no way deserving of it and we have offended him far more often and more deeply than anyone could ever offend us. Yet, he chose to die on the cross so that we could experience abundant life and that our joy may be full (John 10:10; 15:11).

Self-expectations also may have to be adjusted to keep bitterness at bay. If we believe we deserve the best that life has to offer, we are going to be sadly disappointed. For one thing, life on this earth is not all sunshine and roses, nor did God ever promise it would be. In fact, he promised just the opposite.

Perhaps no disappointed expectations are more devastating than our expectations of God. When God doesn't act in the way we think he should, when he doesn't answer our prayers in our timing or in accordance with our plans (we all know that type of prayer: *God, I've decided to do/have/be this. Now please bless it!*), and when God doesn't 'come through' for us, we begin to doubt his love, his goodness, his care for us and his wisdom. That can lead to bitterness and regrets. The book of Ruth describes just such a woman and just such an experience.

Ruth's mother-in-law, Naomi, had certainly had her hopes and dreams dashed by the harsh realities of life. Like most women, she had planned to get married, have children and live happily ever after. She did get married, she did have two sons and both of them married. But then the unexpected happened — her husband and both her sons died. Now she was a distraught widow with two equally distraught daughters-in-law, Orpah and Ruth. Naomi's reaction to the tragedies in her life was to declare: 'The LORD's hand has gone out against me!' (Ruth 1:13). She returned to her home town Bethlehem, with Ruth, and upon their arrival, she was greeted by name. But she replied, 'Don't call me Naomi. Call me Mara [the Hebrew word for "bitter"], because the Almighty has made my life very bitter' (Ruth 1:20).

Naomi must have felt completely abandoned by God. Worse, she may have felt he was persecuting her. Little did she know that all the tragedy in her life had a magnificent purpose and was all part of his glorious plan for her, her family and, ultimately, for billions of people through the ages. Ruth was to marry again. She became the wife of the prosperous Boaz who cared for both of them for the rest of their lives. Ruth had a son, Obed, whose grandson was King David, and from that line came Jesus Christ, born in the little town of Bethlehem, the town to which Naomi returned in bitterness. God used her bitter experiences to bless her and all the world with the coming of the Messiah, the Redeemer of the sins of the world.

God sometimes uses our experiences, our sin, our sorrow, our tragedies, and yes, even our bitterness, to bring to pass his perfect and holy plans and purposes. Naomi had no way of knowing that what she saw as God's failure to protect and prosper her would lead to the coming of the Savior of the world.

Hezekiah had a similar experience. When the prophet Isaiah informed him that God would not heal his disease and that God would, in fact, demand his life, Hezekiah's disappointment with God's plan poured forth: '"Remember, O Lord, how I have walked before you faithfully and with wholehearted devotion and have done what is good in your eyes." And Hezekiah wept bitterly.' But when God showed him mercy and extended his life another fifteen years, Hezekiah understood 'the rest of the story': 'Behold, it was for my welfare that I had great bitterness; but in love you have delivered my life from the pit of destruction, for you have cast all my sins behind your back' (Isa. 38:17, ESV). Sometimes sorrow, grief and bitter experiences are part of God's holy and perfect plan for us. Whatever his purposes for us, we have to hold on to one great truth: '"For I know the plans I have for you," declares the Lord, "plans to prosper you and not to harm you, plans to give you hope and a future"' (Jer. 29:11).

The ultimate root killer

Anyone with a lawn or garden knows how difficult it is to keep them free of weeds. When my husband mows the lawn, he lops the heads off the weeds along with cutting the grass, and for a day or two the lawn looks great. But looks are deceiving. In no time, the weeds grow and some can spread their tentacles across the lawn, putting down more roots everywhere. The only cure is a healthy dose of weed killer, left on long enough to penetrate down to the roots. Our self-effort to rid ourselves of bitterness is a lot like the lawn mower. We may be able to cut off the head of the root, the part that is visible to others, but if the root is still there, it will bring forth the fruit of bitterness again. That root needs to be destroyed just as weed killer destroys the roots of the weeds. On our own, we simply don't have the power to kill the root of bitterness. Only God has that power. We have to ask him to do what we cannot — tear up the root of bitterness and replace it with joy and peace in our hearts. Pray that the Holy Spirit, who resides in your heart, will bring forth *his* fruit. Immerse yourself in his Word and let it do its work in your heart, sanctifying you, as Jesus promised in John 17:17. This is the only way to rid ourselves of the root of bitterness. As my husband so succinctly put it: 'The ultimate weed killer is the Word of God in the hands of the Holy Spirit.'

10

Enough is never enough:

Envy

Little Joey was a great kid and his dad's favorite. He had many older brothers and while his father loved them too, there was something about little Joey that drew his father's heart to him. Dad gave many gifts to all his children, but he gave Joey a special jacket that was the envy of his siblings. Every time he wore that jacket, the brothers both admired it and resented it at the same time. Maybe they wanted jackets of their own. Or maybe they just wished their father had preferred them to Joey. Whatever it was that was eating at them, nothing good was going to come of it. They began to hate Joey and spoke very harshly to him.

When Joey got a little older, he started having some weird dreams and, as kids do, he told his family about them. The odd part about his dreams was that Joey was always the hero in them, the star and the most important one, even though he was young and his brothers were older and stronger. As Joey related his dreams of being the center of attention and admiration, his brothers regarded him through the slit eyes of envy and their hatred for him increased. One day when they were in the park, the brothers grabbed Joey and tossed him into a hole they had dug. They left him there, took his jacket, covered it in mud, and told their father Joey had been in an accident and had been killed. So great was their envy of Joey that not only were they willing to do him great harm, they were also willing to cause their own father agony and grief.

Of course we recognize this as the story of Joseph and the ten older sons of Jacob from the book of Genesis. The setting has been changed, but the motivations of the brothers remain the same — envy, jealousy and the hatred and horrible acts they can lead to. Envy, jealousy and covetousness are very closely related. Envy and jealousy are aimed at people. Covetousness is aimed at their possessions. But envy has an added component; it wishes harm or evil toward the one who has aroused jealousy. Covetousness and jealousy both desire what another has, but envy adds ill-will against him as well. Those who envy not only want what another has, they also want that person to suffer in some way for having it. Envy goes beyond casting a longing glance at the neighbor's new car. That longing, once dwelled upon, can lead to feelings of hatred for the neighbor herself.

Such was the case of Joseph's brothers. Just taking Joseph's 'coat of many colors' (Genesis 37:3, KJV) would not have been enough. They wanted him to suffer for being their father's favorite, despite the fact that Joseph was not responsible for his father's preferential treatment of him. This is what makes envy such a damaging, deadly emotion. Even more destructive than anger and bitterness, envy eats away at us from the inside out.

'A heart at peace gives life to the body, but envy rots the bones' (Prov. 14:30). Joseph's brothers simply couldn't stand the fact that he had more than they did — more of their father's love, more respect and esteem, more of God's blessings, and it rotted their bones. In short, their dissatisfaction was the same as that of all who envy; they were not content with who they were and what they had. They wanted more because they believed they deserved more.

The sad part about envying others for what they have, what they are, or what they do is even if we could have all that they have, we would *never* be satisfied with it, because there will always be someone else to envy or something else to covet. That is the nature of sin. It is never satisfied. The diabolical nature of envy should be obvious. As long as we're chasing after what Satan is dangling in front of us like a carrot in front of a mule, we won't be seeking after God or hungering and thirsting for righteousness (Matt. 5:6). As long as we're looking for joy in obtaining possessions, we cannot be seeking the satisfaction that only Christ provides. As long as we are looking with the green eyes of jealousy at our neighbors' possessions, we will never see them as either brothers and sisters in Christ or lost souls in need of him. As long as we are counting others' blessings instead of our own, we are doomed to be joyless and frustrated. And in all these situations, Satan has the victory.

Women begin their journey in the world of envy very early in life. Of course all children envy what other kids have. Joseph's brothers envied his position as their father's favorite and despised him for it. As girls reach the junior high and high school age, the things we envy center around attractiveness, while boys tend to envy one another for athletic ability. The natural insecurities so common in the early teen years cause us to look through the 'slit eyes of jealousy' at other girls. The ones with silky, shiny hair remind us that ours is mousy or frizzy or dull. The image of the perfect bodies that some have haunts us each time we look in the mirror. Their white teeth, perfect smiles, rosy complexions, perky breasts, long shapely legs and exquisite wardrobes only magnify our shortcomings. We see only our zits, flat chests, fat thighs and Walmart clothes, and of course we come up short by comparison. So we follow the 'perfect girls' on Facebook, talk about them with our friends, and do everything in our power to get close to them and become part of their clique. And if we succeed, we do all in our power to make sure no other girl gets in. The envious desire to belong becomes an envious hatred of anyone who would present competition and possibly threaten our position.

As we mature out of the teen years, envy takes on new goals and hearts begin to tangle in a profound way. We still look with the green eyes of jealousy at other women, but now we see them as competition in the husband market. Here again, attractiveness is huge. Not only are we still competing with other women to be prettier and slimmer, but we have the added pressure of being more of a 'catch' for the men in our circle. Groups of college age and older single women who 'hang out' together with single men have a constant sense of needing to outshine the others in order to catch the eye of the eligible men in the group. Added to this mix is the spiritual component. Not only do we have to be more attractive physically and socially, but we have to subtly present to the men the future prospect of the perfect Christian wife, one who will be acceptable to his family, make him proud at church, and raise perfect Christian children who will be a credit to him. Because of this pressure, we constantly measure ourselves against all other eligible women and the temptation to envy them for their assets, especially in the areas we feel we are lacking, can be overwhelming.

Once we are married and begin our families, envy takes on new targets. Diane's husband has a better job and makes more money. Lynn's kids are really bright and excelling in school. Kasey just bought a new house in an upmarket part of town, professionally decorated and complete with all the latest gadgets. And Jennifer's husband just bought her a brand new SUV with video and a mini fridge! And so it goes. What we often don't realize about those we envy is that they are painfully aware of their own shortcomings and looking at others with longing. Sure Diane's husband makes a lot of money, but he's never home and hardly knows his kids; and she envies Rachel, whose husband works from home. Lynn's children may be doing well in school, but how often do they feel so much pressure to excel that learning becomes drudgery? How she wishes they could be as carefree and fun-loving as Debbie's kids. That new house of Kasey's looks great, but it probably has saddled her with a thirty-year mortgage and huge payments that stretch her budget to the limit. She envies her parents who paid off their mortgage years ago. And Jennifer's SUV lost half its value as soon as they drove it away from the dealers, and a year from now, she'll be looking with envy at her neighbor driving the newest model.

Even in church, we envy other women for their gifts and talents. Lisa sings so beautifully, Ashley teaches fifty women in a Bible study, Lindsey's kids win awards for the number of Bible verses they memorize, Jessica's husband is an elder. We want what they have and we resent them for having it. This is the subtle and sinister nature of envy. It is never satisfied. Never.

The culture of envy

[Much of modern marketing is designed to feed our envy of what others have and stir up discontent with what we have.] Unhappy with your husband? Read this book. Unhappy with your appearance? Buy this machine, this diet or this self-help book. Bored with life? Try this vacation spot, this makeover. Marketing convinces us that if only we buy whatever it is they are selling, it will make us happier, richer, prettier, younger-looking, more successful, more up to date, better parents. We need to have bigger homes, fancier cars, nicer clothes, whiter teeth, more apps on our Iphones, faster internet service, wider broadband, more cable channels. [It's an endless barrage of 'stuff' designed to feed our discontent with our husbands, our looks, our homes, our status in the world, and so on.]

But when we give in to our hunger for the world's goods and buy them, they are quickly obsolete, out of date, out of fashion. Planned obsolescence is part of the plot. Nothing is built to last or designed to meet our needs completely. How else can they get us to go back and get the new, improved model? Once we have it, whatever 'it' is, we are not satisfied with it and immediately desire something else. Hence, the West is comprised of the most overdressed, overfed, overindulged and over-indebted nations in the history of the world.

God knows this part of the sin nature very well, which is why the Tenth Commandment deals with envy and covetousness. 'You shall not covet your neighbor's house; you shall not covet your neighbor's wife, nor his male servant, nor his female servant, nor his ox, nor his donkey, nor anything that is your neighbor's' (Exod. 20:17). God knew that the tendency to envy and covet is just as much part of the sin nature we inherited from Adam as the inclination to lie, steal, commit adultery and murder. All spring from a discontent with what we have and a deeply held conviction that we deserve better. Another name for that conviction is pride. Our pride leads us to grieve over others' possessions and achievements as reminders of our own lack of them. *I'm just as good as so-and-so, maybe even better than her. So why does she have more than I do?* Pride tells us that we deserve the best of everything, which is one reason why the 'health, wealth and prosperity' gospel is so popular. It feeds our pride, our envy, and our deep-seated desire to elevate ourselves above others.

As Christian women, we simply must learn to discern between what the world, including worldly philosophies and religions that tangle our hearts, has to offer and what God offers through Christ. It is only when we hunger and thirst after righteousness that we will be completely filled and satisfied (Matt. 5:6). He never goes out of style, never becomes obsolete. Christ is the Bread of Life and the Living Water that fills completely. Only he satisfies. The New Testament identifies covetousness as a form of idolatry, a sin which God detests: 'Put to death, therefore, whatever belongs to your earthly nature: sexual immorality, impurity, lust, evil desires and greed, which is idolatry' (Col. 3:5). But the culture we live in, especially in the West, turns upside down the truth of the Scriptures. Greed is not only acceptable; it's encouraged. Let's face it. Greed and envy are good for business.

The evil of envy

The Bible is full of envious people. Not one of them is presented in a positive light and things didn't go well for any of them.

Cain committed the first murder out of envy for Abel. Envious of their God-ordained position, Korah led a rebellion against Moses and Aaron which resulted in the deaths of thousands of Israelites (Num. 16). King Saul so envied David's popularity with the people that he looked at him with a spiteful, malicious, envious eye (1 Sam. 18:9) and tried numerous times to kill him. Haman's jealousy of Mordecai's favor with the king resulted in his gruesome death on the gallows he had prepared for Mordecai (Esth. 5:9, 12-13; 7:10). The princes of Babylon were so envious of Daniel's exceptional qualities that they trumped up charges against him and had him thrown in a pit with lions, where God miraculously saved him. For their plot, those who had falsely accused Daniel were themselves devoured by the lions (Dan. 6).

Most heinous of all were the chief priests whose envy led them to hand Jesus over to the Romans to be crucified (Matt. 27:18). Jesus' popularity with the people was a slap in the face of their pride and ambition. That spirit of envy led the same element among the Jewish leaders to jail the Apostles (Acts 5:17-18), to rail against Paul and Barnabas (Acts 13:45), and to excite the mobs against Paul and Silas (Acts 17:5).

The hatred of the religious leaders for Jesus is described in the parable of the workers in the vineyard (Matt. 20:1-16). The first group of workers in the parable were those who had worked an entire day and resented receiving the same wage as the last group who only worked for an hour. Their attitude was similar to that of the Pharisees who were incensed at Jesus' teaching that others could inherit a heavenly kingdom they thought was reserved for them alone. They despised Jesus for offering the kingdom to poor, oppressed, weak sinners whom he made equal to them. In verse 15, the landowner asks: 'Is your eye evil because

I am good?' The 'evil eye' was a Hebrew expression referring to jealousy and envy. God's goodness and mercy produced in the self-righteous Pharisees the evil eye of envy. It is that same 'evil eye' that infects us today, as we look at the blessings bestowed on others as threats to our own confidence and well-being.

Putting off envy

Envy is a hideous, ugly sin and there is no place for it in the heart of a Christian. If we don't recognize it and confess it for what it is, it takes root in our hearts and leads to worse sins. Why do people steal if not because they envy what someone else has? Why do we secretly gloat when a rich and famous person falls upon hard times if not because we envy their wealth and privilege? If it were not for the innate envy found in every human heart, the Hollywood gossipmongers would be out of a job. Have you ever noticed that the glee with which they report the breakup of a Hollywood marriage far exceeds the joy with which they reported the wedding in the first place? Envy is characteristic of Christ's rejecters, not Christ's followers. It leads to estrangement from God (Rom. 1:28-29) and even to murder (James 4:2).

When we struggle with envy (and who doesn't?), we must first recognize that it grieves God and damages our relationship with him. Our desire to be rid of the sin of envy is the first step to yielding to the Spirit's power to do away with it. It is also what distinguishes us from non-Christians. We may envy and covet just as much as they do, but unlike them, we see it as sin and we hate it. Envy is powerful and pervasive and no sin of the flesh can be conquered by efforts of the flesh. It is only conquered by the Spirit. We increase the Spirit's influence in our lives and we appropriate his power by increasing our time in his Word and in prayer. These are the only weapons powerful enough to conquer the spirit of envy. 'Therefore, laying aside all malice, all deceit, hypocrisy, envy, and all evil speaking, as newborn babes, desire the pure milk of the word, that you may grow thereby' (1 Peter 2:1-2, NKJV).

11

Three truths about negative emotions

A place to start

There are three important truths about negative emotions to use as starting points in dealing with them. Before we begin this discussion, however, a word of caution is in order. Some women reading this chapter may have a very negative response to some of it, a very negative *emotional* response. To those women, I simply say *please keep reading,* even though your first impulse may be to toss the book into the trash. The dilemma faced in a book like this is how to talk to women biblically about their harmful negative emotions without them having a negative emotional reaction to the truths presented. Just like those math students, once the emotions take over, rational thought tends to go out of the window. But by saying upfront that there may very well be a negative emotional response to this analysis of women's emotions, hopefully readers can be on guard against the offense that so often arises in women when we speak of our emotions. Having said that, let's look at the three truths about negative emotions.

First, negative emotions do *not* have power over us. So many women believe they simply have to live at the mercy of their emotions and there's nothing that can be done about them. Not true. If God says, 'Do not fear,' that means that through the power of the Holy Spirit, we have the capacity to not fear. If he says, 'Don't be angry,' that means that anger can be defeated, again by the Spirit's power. But too many Christian women live in the grip of their emotions, often declaring: 'That's just the way I am. I can't help it!' So they go on being fearful, doubting, angry and guilty because they believe they are stuck with who and what they are. They give in and give up and consign themselves to living at the mercy of their emotions because those feelings are so powerful they seem to be uncontrollable. This is just one more of Satan's lies designed to keep us in bondage to our sin nature and keep us out of the spiritual battle.

The woman who believes her emotions are all powerful has forgotten another of God's truths. When we come to Christ, he recreates us into an entirely new person. 'Therefore, if anyone is in Christ, he is a *new creation*; the old has gone, the new has come!' (2 Cor. 5:17, emphasis added). Jesus doesn't simply give us new spiritual clothing to put over our old selves. He strips us bare, scrubs us clean inside and out, and puts on us the pure white garments of his holiness and righteousness. The Holy Spirit comes into our new hearts and resides there for ever, enabling us by his power to 'do all things through Christ who strengthens' us (Phil. 4:13). He enables us to be 'more than conquerors through him who loved us' (Rom. 8:37). No negative emotion or thought can withstand his power.

To be a 'conqueror' means to have total victory over the enemy, and for most women, negative emotions are our worst enemy.

140

But when we are in Christ, he is the victor, not our feelings. Our emotions do not have the power to subdue us. We don't have to settle for living in bondage to them, crying, '*It's just the way I am*,' because it really isn't the way we are any more. We've been made new creations in Christ and have the power to subdue our emotions and dictate to them rather than living at their mercy. Of course there are still battles with our feelings, but the Holy Spirit within us empowers us to win those battles as we buckle on the belt of God's truth and use the shield of faith to ward off the blows of Satan's flaming arrows aimed at our emotions.

The second truth regarding emotions is when God commands us to believe and not doubt and to fear not, etc., he is commanding us to act, not feel. He doesn't say, 'I want you to feel loving toward others.' He says, 'Love one another.' That's an action. Action is a result of the will overriding emotion. Emotions will respond to the will eventually, but like children or animals that need training, it takes time. We take the time to train our children to act in certain ways and resist acting in other ways, don't we? If we train our emotions to behave in the way our wills dictate, instead of the other way around, we can stop living by our emotions and start living by the faith we have been given, which is why we have to start by being sure of our salvation.

We will act out what we think because we believe what we think.

But this is not to say that any amount of training will cause our emotions to disappear. The goal is not to stifle our emotional nature, but to bring it under the control of our new natures in Christ. The old nature, the one that causes us to be undone by our emotions, is no longer in command. Realizing that simple truth goes a long way to enabling us to respond to negative emotions in a positive way. As we grow and mature in Christ, the new nature he has given us curbs our tendency to act and react to destructive emotional forces and enables us to look at those forces through the lens of truth. We can then allow that truth to shape our thoughts and actions, regardless of how we feel. Then when our emotions say, 'Do this,' or 'Come to this conclusion,' we can say, 'No, I'm going to choose to do the opposite because God's Word says it's the best for me. And I want to please him by obeying.' What does this presuppose? That we know God and know his Word. This too is part of the battle. Everything and everyone will get in the way of you and God and time in the Word. But time in the Word is the only way to know him and love him and want to obey him. It's also the only way to feed and strengthen the new nature within us.

The third truth we must understand about negative emotions to use as starting points in order to deal with them is the really hard part, which is why I began this chapter with a warning. I said there would be some parts of this discussion that would be difficult to hear and many women would react emotionally to some of these statements. This is especially true of this third truth. Ready? Here it is: we simply have to accept that many of these negative emotions are sin because God commands against them.

Of course there are fears, doubts and feelings of guilt that are not sin, and God certainly does not command against them. The fear of jumping off a ten-storey building is not a sin; it's a life-saving device that God has graciously built within us. Doubts about the outrageous claims by the health, wealth and prosperity purveyors are certainly not sinful; these are healthy doubts that warn us of spiritual danger. Feelings of guilt over some cruel or thoughtless words we have used to hurt others are legitimate and drive us to make amends; feelings of guilt over past sins that were nailed to the cross of Christ are not. But if God commands against certain things, this means they are choices and they can be chosen against. To choose to experience or live under the influence of things God commands against is to commit the sin of disobedience and unbelief. There's just no escaping that conclusion.

This is a hard thing to come to grips with, isn't it? As women, our emotions are such a huge part of who we are. But they are also what get our hearts tangled into a jumbled mess. Even if we resist the idea that negative emotions are sin, and many women do resist it, we still can accept that they are harmful for us. And aren't the things God commands against *always* harmful for us? God declares something to be sin, not because he just wants to spoil our fun, but because the things that are sinful are bad for us, make us unhappy and spoil our lives. So accept that fear, doubt, anger, envy and the rest are sin because they go against God's Word and hurt us. God loves us enough to want the best for us and what damages us isn't what's best for us. That's why we have to accept that these negative emotions are sin and deal with them accordingly, by the power of the Holy Spirit. And dealing with them begins with the three things just mentioned: emotions do not have power over us; we do have choices. God commands us to act, not feel. If God commands against negative emotions, continuing willfully in them is sin.

For many women, untangling the heart begins with taking a long, hard look at the emotions that drive us. Take some time to get alone with God and ask him to reveal the state of your emotions to you in a clear way so you can begin to deal with them. But there is one emotion that should rule in our hearts and that is the love of God who 'has poured out his love into our hearts by the Holy Spirit, whom he has given us' (Rom. 5:5). Negative emotions are no match for the power of that great love.

12

Refuse to think about yourself:

Martyn-Lloyd Jones's timeless advice

Christian biographer Iain Murray, in his account of the famous Welsh preacher, Dr Martyn Lloyd-Jones, writes that Lloyd-Jones was as well known for his counseling as for his extraordinary sermons. Many Christians of his day have testified to the practical effects of his counsel. A woman who had received conflicting advice from others gives this statement of the counsel she received from Lloyd-Jones: 'His five-word prescription was unbelievably simple, though he well knew it was the hardest thing for me to do. What were those five words? *Refuse to think about yourself.*'

She goes on to say, 'I felt like Naaman shattered by his instructions from Elisha, but like him, as I obeyed, I found release and gradual healing.' Naaman was the mighty commander of the Syrian army who suffered from leprosy and was told to go to Elisha, the great prophet in Israel, for healing (2 Kings 5). Elisha told him to wash himself seven times in the Jordan and his response was: 'Huh!

I thought he would come out and wave his hand over me and cure the leprosy', and he went away angry. But eventually he obeyed and was healed. Lloyd-Jones's five-word 'cure' seemed to this woman too simple, but she realized in her obedience that it was more profound than she could imagine. It is even more profound, and even more needed, today than ever.

So the fourth in our five-point cure for a tangled heart is Martyn Lloyd-Jones's advice: Refuse to think about yourself. There is one inviolable rule in life and if you remember nothing else from this book, remember this: 'Those who obsess about themselves will never be happy in any circumstance. Those who obsess about God will find joy in all circumstances.' When our thoughts begin with us and end with us — the norm in this unhealthy 'psychological' generation we live in — we will live in a constant state of defeat because we are controlled by subjective feelings centered on ourselves, rather than objective truth centered on God.

For one thing, self-obsessers are those who are continually questioning their relationship with God, not in a practical way, but in a way that gets them into a rut of questioning, but never coming to conclusions. They ask the same questions over and over, always about themselves and their thoughts and doubts and fears. What they really need to do is stop thinking about, and focusing on, themselves and redirect their focus to their God.

Let me tell you a secret. Your greatest enemy is not Satan. It's not the culture and it's not even other people. It's you. You are your worst enemy. And I am my worst enemy. That's because we are the hardest ones for us to control. Paul understood this principle better than anyone. He struggled daily with his flesh, his old nature, that part of all of us that wars continually against the new creation we are in Christ: 'I know that nothing good lives in me, that is, in my sinful nature. For I have the desire to do what is good, but I cannot carry it out. For what I do is not the good I want to do; no, the evil I do not want to do — this I keep on doing' (Rom. 7:18-19). This, too, is part of the battle that is the Christian life, the battle between the new person Jesus created in us and the old person in which the new person must reside. Think of it as bacteria that we are born with and which produce a serious illness. Once an antibiotic is introduced into our bodies, it begins to do battle with the bacteria. Both are trying to control the 'territory' and have dominance. The bacteria strive to weaken and kill us, while the antibiotic works to thwart their plans and produce strength and health in us. Although either the bacteria or the antibiotic eventually gets the victory in the physical battle, the spiritual combat rages on until the end of our lives. Only in heaven is total victory possible. But in the meantime, the two natures within us continue to fight. Refusing to think about ourselves involves choosing to stop obsessing about the old person we once were and focus on the new person which is Christ within us.

Dead and gone

What we continually forget, if we ever learned it in the first place, is that we are dead. Galatians 2:20 says, 'I have been crucified with Christ and I no longer live, but Christ lives in me. The life I live in the body, I live by faith in the Son of God, who loved me and gave himself for me.' What this is saying is that the person you were before you came to Christ is dead, and the person who walks around in your body is Christ. Just remember that the Christian life is one of death to self and rising to 'walk in the newness of life' (Rom. 6:4), and that new life is characterized by thoughts about him who saved us, not thoughts about the dead flesh that has been crucified with Christ. An ancient Roman punishment is said to be tying the corpse of a murdered man to the back of his murderer. As the corpse decayed and rotted, it would infect the living man until he became ill and died. When we are continually thinking about ourselves, and especially our past hurts and experiences, we are essentially obsessing about a corpse, full of rottenness and death. Why would we want to do that? We are new creations in Christ. 'If anyone is in Christ, he is a new creation; the old has gone, the new has come!' (2 Cor. 5:17). The old person you were, with all its sin and the misery and pain that accompanies sin, is gone, dead, over, for ever. Don't keep bringing it back to life. Don't keep digging up the coffin. Don't keep rehashing old hurts that produce bitterness, and old mistakes that produce guilt and regret. If God has saved you out of a cesspool, don't dive back in and swim around.

Why, then, do we still struggle if the old person is dead? Primarily, it's because we don't truly believe it's really dead. And because we still sin, our minds are continually drawn back to the sinful nature. Part of the blame is again on the demon-controlled culture we live in. They do everything in their power to keep our focus on our old selves, appealing to the lusts of the eyes and flesh, and the pride of life. They constantly present temptations to dwell on ourselves, not on the new selves we are in Christ, but on the old selves which were in bondage. You see, Satan doesn't give up his servants without a fight. His efforts to keep his hold on us are reminiscent of the last scene in the movie *Carrie* where a girl dreams she is standing in a graveyard looking at Carrie's tombstone, thankful and relieved that the evil Carrie is dead and buried. But suddenly a hand comes up through the dirt of the grave and grabs her ankle. Satan is like Carrie; he doesn't want to let us go and when we walk through his graveyard by obsessing about our dead selves, he is there to grab our ankles and drag us down.

The death of self

All those negative emotions we talked about are the product of turning inwardly. Fear, doubt, guilt, anger, bitterness, envy — all are self-focused. But their opposites, the positive emotions, are all outwardly focused on God. Confidence and strength, the opposites of fear, come from our trust in God. Faith, the opposite of doubt, is a gift from God and focuses on him. Forgiveness, the opposite of guilt, is another gift from God and allows us to focus outwardly on forgiving others. Love, joy, peace and contentment are the opposites of anger, bitterness and envy, and they are fruits of the Spirit, products of the Spirit's work in the new creations we are. Thinking about the love of God who sent Jesus to die for us makes it impossible to be angry and bitter toward others. Thinking on, and being grateful for, the peace and contentment we have in our new selves makes it impossible to envy.

When our feelings and thoughts are primarily about ourselves, we can never overcome our problems and untangle our hearts. If your world is falling apart, it's because it's *your* world. The kingdom of God never falls apart and we are citizens of that kingdom, where God is the ruler. As long as you are parked firmly on the throne of your life, you're going to have problems, simply because you're not supposed to be there. The throne of your life is God's throne. Your place is on your knees before it. It's all a matter of perspective. It's not all about you, despite what Satan tells you through the culture. It's God's throne, not yours. Don't believe the same old lie he's been telling since the Garden in Genesis 3:15: *Eat the fruit. You'll be like God!* No, you won't.

Furthermore, you will never get rid of your fears and doubts by thinking about your fears and doubts. This is why God calls us to focus on him and the great doctrines of the faith and their relevance to life: the love, grace and mercy of God, the reality of our relationship with Christ who died for us and gave us new life, the promise of the Holy Spirit who indwells us, and the hope of eternal glory. Understanding these great truths, centering our thoughts on them, and going over them in our minds will enable us to reason from truth in all of life's trials, and our faith will be strong and vital. Reasoning from what we feel about ourselves — rather than what we know about God — is the sure path to spiritual defeat.

But it is sadly true that some women don't want to change this part of their lives. It's who they are, it's their identity, and trying to get them to lose their identity is very difficult. Their hearts are tangled with thoughts and feelings centered on themselves, and it has become a very powerful, deeply-ingrained habit. Jesus said, 'Out of the overflow of the heart the mouth speaks' (Matt. 12:34). When we hear women constantly talking about themselves — their experiences, their past, their thoughts, their feelings, their problems — that is an indication that their hearts are filled with *them* and the abundance of self-focused thoughts spills over into their conversations. What we love, what we value, what we revere and worship will always show up in our conversations.

149

Remember when you were in love? You couldn't stop talking about the beloved. He filled your heart and mind day and night; he was all you thought about and all you talked about. That's the way we should feel and talk about Christ, our beloved, our Bridegroom. But if our minds are set on *us*, then *we* are all we talk about because *we* are all we're truly interested in. The culture of greed we live in encourages just this kind of thinking because when we are obsessing about ourselves, the inevitable result is discontent. And what do we do when we are discontented? We shop. We eat. We fill our lives with entertainment. Of course we find no cure for our discontentment in these things, which keeps us going back for more. This is the result of self focus. The carnal self, the old person, is never satisfied. We have to stop feeding it. The opening words to the song 'Satisfied' describe the result of feeding the old self:

> All my life long I had panted,
> For a drink from some cool spring,
> That I hoped would quench the burning
> Of the thirst I felt within.
> Feeding on the husks around me,
> Till my strength was almost gone,
> Longed my soul for something better,
> Only still to hunger on.
> Poor I was, and sought for riches,
> Something that would satisfy,
> But the dust I gathered round me
> Only mocked my soul's sad cry.

The 'husks' we feed on are the pathetic, dried up, worthless empty shells of what Satan and the world offer us, the kind of things we pursued before we died with Christ and were resurrected with him. They sapped our spiritual strength and left us hungry, thirsty and sad. Then we were born again:

> Well of water, ever springing,
> Bread of life so rich and free,
> Untold wealth that never faileth,
> My Redeemer is to me.
> Hallelujah! I have found Him
> Whom my soul so long has craved!
> Jesus satisfies my longings,
> Through His blood I now am saved.

The new nature, Christ in us, will never be satisfied by the things of the world. Only Jesus satisfies our longings. Talking and thinking about ourselves is just feeding on the husks of death. But the Spirit within us leaps for joy when he hears us talk about him! Just like John the Baptist leapt for joy in his mother's womb when he heard the voice of the Savior's mother, so the Spirit who lives in our hearts floods us with joy when we read his Word, talk about him, think about him. The only one who is joyful when we obsess about ourselves is Satan.

It is so clear that we absolutely must refocus our thinking away from ourselves if our hearts are to be untangled from the things that encumber it. You're dead. Face it. So stop obsessing about the corpse and obsess about the new life Christ has provided for you by his death on the cross. That's where true joy is. Refuse to think about yourself!

13

The universe next door:

Focusing on our magnificent God

When I speak at women's retreats, I do an exercise to demonstrate the fifth and final step in untangling the heart. I ask the women to close their eyes and think of anything except a purple elephant. Then I tell them to open their eyes and I ask how many were thinking about a purple elephant. Most raise their hands. Then I ask them to close their eyes and think of Pikes Peak, the magnificent 14,000-foot mountain that rises above our Colorado town. They are to think about any view they've ever seen of the mountain, whether bathed in the morning sunlight, or blanketed in snow in winter, or reflecting the golden glow of the aspen trees that cover its lower slopes. Once they have that image fixed in their minds, I ask them to open their eyes and tell me how many were thinking of purple elephants. Rarely does anyone raise her hand. This illustrates the fifth of our five principles for untangling the heart: when we try to rid ourselves of harmful thought patterns without replacing them with beneficial ones, we are doomed to fail.

If you take to heart Lloyd-Jones's admonition to refuse to think about yourself, you can't simply say to yourself, 'I'm not going to think about myself. I'm not going to think about myself.' Why doesn't that work? Because you're thinking about not thinking about yourself, so that's what you end up thinking about. It's like the purple elephant. Trying not to think about it didn't work for the women. It was only when they conjured up images of the beauty and magnificence of Pikes Peak that thoughts about the elephant went away.

Negative thought patterns which tangle our hearts can easily become an ingrained habit. We need to replace the negative thoughts with positive thoughts about God and his truth. I've heard from many people, both men and women, wanting to know how to rid themselves of harmful thoughts. They obsess about getting rid of the harmful thoughts and think of nothing else. Of course they're failing, because they are thinking about the very things they're trying not to think about. I never tell them how to forget their thoughts. I tell them to redirect their thoughts to God and fill their minds with him; then the harmful thoughts will go away by themselves.

Ephesians 4:22-24 describes the path to victory over bad habits of negative thoughts and doubts. Replace them. 'You were taught, with regard to your former way of life, to put off your old self, which is being corrupted by its deceitful desires; to be made new in the attitude of your minds, and to put on the new self, created to be like God in true righteousness and holiness.' Paul goes on to exhort those who are in Christ to 'put off' the old self with its deceit and corruption and 'put on' the new self with its righteousness. Put off lying and put on truthfulness. Put off stealing and put on usefulness and work. Put off bitterness, rage and anger, and put on kindness, compassion and forgiveness. See the pattern? It's the same thing we see in Romans 12:2. Paul doesn't simply say, 'Do not conform any longer to the pattern of this world' and leave it there. He adds: 'but be transformed by the renewing of your mind.' Replacing the negatives we put off with the positives we put on is absolutely essential.

Paul's admonition to you is that *you are a new woman in Christ; now live like it by deliberately rejecting the habits that characterized your old life and replacing them with new habits.* Those old habits are thoughts centered on you and all the things that go with it — obsessing about fears and doubts, analyzing feelings, scrutinizing others' words and actions toward you. The new habits are the spiritual disciplines of prayer, Bible study, Christian fellowship (with real Christians who want to talk about God, not about themselves), meditation, public worship. God has given us these things not as a luxury but as a spiritual necessity. Just as food, water and air are necessities of the physical life, so are the Bread of Life, Living Water and the Holy Spirit necessities of the spiritual life. We must utilize these resources or we will suffer spiritually and our hearts will remain tangled. We simply cannot live without them and we certainly can't fight the good fight without them.

Replacing thoughts of ourselves with thoughts of God is part of the fight. So put off fear and put on confidence and strength. Put off doubt and put on faith. Put off guilt and put on the joy of forgiveness. Put off bitterness and put on peace and love. Put off anger and put on gentleness, kindness and love. Are these things really possible for us? Absolutely. If they weren't, then God would be lying to us in his Word. Do you think God is lying to us? Of course not.

Putting off

So how do we begin to 'put off' negative emotions and thoughts of self? Where do we start? Some people would say we should start with God's love. But I tell you that there are more words spoken about the love of God, more books written on the subject and more sermons preached on the love of God than any other topic. Why, then, are women still anxious, depressed, doubting and fearful? Because the love of God is not real to us. For one thing, we don't understand the true biblical concept of love. Our idea of love gets all tangled up with romance and feelings. That is not *agape* love.

I believe that, without exception, the first order of business in the untangling of hearts is to sharpen focus on the sovereignty of God. A high view of God is the ultimate solution to every heart-entangling complexity of life. Faith falters and the flesh prevails when people lose a biblical perspective on the nature of God. To be reminded that he is 'in his holy temple', ruling and reigning in sovereign majesty, ordering and superintending the affairs of his world with actual hands-on management so that not a sparrow falls to the ground without his notice, is the food that strengthens faith. How reassuring it is to know that Psalm 31:15 is true in our lives: 'My times are in his hand'! My good times and my bad times; my happy times and my sad times; my times of employment and times of unemployment; my times of popularity and times of persecution; my times of health and times of sickness; my times of wealth and times of want; my times of companionship and times of loneliness — all are in his hands. Nothing is more encouraging than to know that all of our times, everything that happens in our lives, is either ordained by him or allowed by him for his own perfect purpose.

Through his sovereign control, he is able to overrule even the wicked actions of men for the good of his children and the glory of his name. Indeed, helping ourselves and helping other hurting souls starts here — knowing God intimately, his nature, his attributes, revealed in the ageless, timeless, infallible truths of the Scriptures. He is the source of everything we need to untangle our hearts, and our hearts will untangle directly proportional to our time in the Word.

The Pilgrim's Progress is a wonderful depiction of the Christian life. In one part, the hero, Christian, and Hopeful, his companion, take a short cut on their way to the Celestial City (heaven). They are captured by the Giant Despair and put in a dungeon in Doubting Castle. There they languish, doubting and despairing, until they realize they have had the key to unlocking the prison door all along — the promises of God which they forgot when they went off the path. God's Word is full of his promises: promises that will encourage us, free us, thrill us and bring us joy; but only if we camp out there and fill our hearts with its truths.

Putting on

How vital it is for those with tangled hearts to think clearly about God, to know him and his attributes. He is a righteous, holy God who will not allow an injustice to continue for ever. He is a faithful God who always keeps his promises. 'If we are faithless, he will remain faithful, for he cannot disown himself' (2 Tim. 2:13). It's one thing to know what the Bible says about God's faithfulness to fulfill his promises, but it's another to act upon them and live according to them. When Tom says he'll be home at 6.00pm, I make dinner for 6.00pm because I know he does what he says he will do. If he doesn't show up at 6.00pm, I don't throw up my hands and say, 'That's it. It's over. I can't trust him. He doesn't love me anymore.' And I certainly don't come to the conclusion that he is unfaithful. I know I can trust him and I know he loves me and I know he's faithful. There's just something about the situation I don't know. He was detained at work, he had a flat tire, he stopped at the store, he lost his watch. But I don't come to wrong conclusions about him, his motives, his love and care for me, or his faithfulness and trustworthiness, because I've been with him long enough to really know him. But when God says he works all things together for good, even cancer, unemployment, rejection and heartache, do we believe him? When he says no trial will be beyond our ability to bear it and he will provide a way out, do we believe that? Or do we try to dig out from under it in our own strength and power? Do we know him well enough to trust him? Jesus told Peter in John 13:7: 'What I am doing you do not understand now, but afterward you will understand.' Can we have enough confidence in God to wait on him? We can if we know him and truly believe that he is faithful.

Ours is a merciful God whose compassions fail not. 'Because of the LORD's great love we are not consumed, for his compassions never fail. They are new every morning; great is your faithfulness' (Lam. 3:22-23). In his compassion and mercy, God sent Jesus and promised that 'A bruised reed he will not break, and a smoldering wick he will not snuff out, till he leads justice to victory' (Matt. 12:20). The smoldering wick is that of a lamp when the oil is exhausted and the flame is flickering and dying. It is a symbol of feebleness and infirmity. Jesus would not further oppress those who had little strength; he would not put out hope and life when it seemed to be almost extinct. Here is a picture of believers who have been bruised and wounded by life's circumstances or other people, and who think God has abandoned them. But that is simply not true. His compassion toward the weak and wounded is unfailing.

He is an unchangeable God who does not waver in his purposes. 'He who is the Glory of Israel does not lie or change his mind; for he is not a man, that he should change his mind' (1 Sam. 15:29). We can have complete confidence that he who has 'set his seal of ownership on us' (2 Cor. 1:22) will never remove his love from us. He will never forsake us, leave us to struggle alone, or grow impatient with us. '"Though the mountains be shaken, and the hills be removed, yet my unfailing love for you will not be shaken nor my covenant of peace be removed," says the LORD, who has compassion on you' (Isa. 54:10). When he says his love is 'everlasting', that's exactly what he means. When he makes a covenant, it doesn't change. His plans are not affected by changing, unfaithful people so that he has to be constantly revising them.

What comfort would it be to pray to one who, like the chameleon who changes color depending on its environment, changed his mind every minute? If God changed, we could not depend on anything his Word says, nor could we call him our Rock. But he is our Rock, like a huge boulder in a stream. The waters go around and over it, but it does not move. The tides ebb and flow, but the Rock remains. In the same way, the tides of human affairs ebb and flow, but God's purpose and will remain unchanged, and his ability to bring them to pass remains unchanged. Not so human beings who change on a whim and upon whom we cannot depend. As the song says, 'Friends may fail me, foes assail me, He, my Savior, makes me whole.'

These are just a few of God's many attributes, the knowledge of which thrills the soul far beyond all earthly joys and imaginings. God's nature and character are limitless and it's only when we fill our minds with him that our hearts are untangled and we lose that which is plaguing our souls. Charles Spurgeon said it best: 'Do you want to lose your sorrows? Do you want to drown your cares? Then plunge yourself into the Godhead's deepest sea and be lost in its immensity.'

A wide range of Christian books is available from EP Books. If you would like a free catalogue please write to us or contact us by e-mail. Alternatively, you can view the whole catalogue online at our web sites.

EP BOOKS
Faverdale North
Darlington
DL3 0PH, England

www.epbooks.org
e-mail: sales@epbooks.org